For players or almost all level

CHRISTOF SIELECKI

Keep It Simple
1.d4

A Solid and Straightforward Chess Opening Repertoire for White

NEW!

NEW IN CHESS

After the success of his award-winning book *Keep it Simple 1.e4*, IM Christof Sielecki is back. His major objective is again to dominate Black from the opening, by simple means.

Sielecki's repertoire with 1.d4 may be even easier to master than his 1.e4 recommendations, because it is such a coherent system: the main concept is for White to play 1.d4, 2.♘f3, 3.g3, 4.♗g2, 5.0-0 and in most cases 6.c4.

The variations are straightforward, easy to remember, and require little or no maintenance. You don't need to sacrifice anything or memorize long tactical lines

Ambitious players rated 1500 or higher will get great value out of studying this extremely accessible book.

paperback | 432 pages | €29.95 | available at your local (chess)bookseller or at newinchess.com | a NEW IN CHESS publication

Tal, Petrosian, Spassky and Korchnoi. *A Chess Multibiography with 207 Games.*

Andrew Soltis. 2019, $65 library binding (18.4 × 26 cm), 394pp., 30 photographs, 207 games, appendices, notes, bibliography, indexes, 978-1-4766-7146-8. Describes the intense rivalry—and collaboration—of the four players who created the golden era when USSR chess players dominated the world. "Arguably the best book Grandmaster Andy Soltis has ever written"—IM John Donaldson. BOOK OF THE YEAR AWARD—*Chess Journalists of America*.

Neumann, Hirschfeld and Suhle.
19th Century Berlin Chess Biographies with 711 Games. Hans Renette *and* Fabrizio Zavata-relli. 2018, $75 library binding (21.9 × 28.5 cm), 382pp., 66 photographs, appendices, notes, bibliography, indexes, 978-1-4766-7379-0. Around 1860 a wave of young Berliners ranked among the world's best. Little has heretofore been written about their lives (richly revealed) and games (analyzed in detail). "Impressive variety of sources...a wonderful achievement"—*American Chess Magazine*; "lively...interesting and enjoyable"—*Mind's Eye Press*.

Kurt Richter. *A Chess Biography with 499 Games.*
Alan McGowan. 2018, $75 library binding (21.9 × 28.5 cm), 380pp., 93 photographs, appendices, notes, bibliography, indexes, 978-1-4766-6906-9. This very large-scale overview of Richter's life (1900–1969) and games sheds light on a sharp and inventive player and influential editor, with much never-before-seen material. "A treasure trove of games and a wonderful overview of the German chess scene of this period! 5 shining stars!"—*New in Chess*; "A model of what a game collection and biography should be....highly recommended"—IM John Donaldson.

The Gijón International Chess Tournaments, 1944–1965.
A History with Biographies and 213 Games. Pedro Méndez Castedo *and* Luis Méndez Castedo. 2019, $45 softcover (17.8 × 25.4 cm), 252pp., 21 photographs, appendices, bibliography, indexes, 978-1-4766-7659-3. Covers the decline of world champion Alekhine and the rise of the child prodigy Arturo Pomar, along with the great chess of Euwe, Rossolimo, Prins, Medina, Larsen and others.

Fred Reinfeld. *The Man Who Taught America Chess.*
Alex Dunne. 2019, $45 softcover (17.8 × 25.4 cm), 276 games, bibliography, index, 978-1-4766-7654-8. Fred Reinfeld's name is known to almost every chess player in the United States. But his accomplishments are not so well known. He was a ranking player, an accomplished author, respected numismatist and an editor or contributor to almost every major chess magazine of the '30s and '40s. "A pioneering work"—IM John Donaldson.

"THINK TWICE!" OIL ON LINEN, LOUIS MUNROE 2019 (dwaynesueno@gmail.com)

Louis Paulsen. *A Chess Biography with 719 Games.*
Hans Renette. 2019, $75 library binding (21.9 × 28.5 cm), 448pp., 108 photographs, 719 games, appendices, notes, bibliography, indexes, 978-1-4766-7195-6. This biography—the first in English—explores Paulsen's career and includes 719 of his games with both contemporary and modern notes. "Definitive...outstanding...highly recommended"—IM John Donaldson.

British Chess Literature to 1914.
A Handbook for Historians. Tim Harding. 2018, $49.95 softcover (17.8 × 25.4 cm), 399 pp., 72 photographs, 23 games, appendices, notes, bibliography, indexes, 978-1-4766-6839-0. Exhaustive coverage of almost 600 chess columns and periodicals from 1813 on and 150 years of books. "Seldom a chess book has impressed so much ...a must have"—*Chessbook Reviews*. BOOK OF THE YEAR AWARD—*Chess Journalists of America*.

A World of Chess. *Its Development and Variations through Centuries and Civilizations.*
Jean-Louis Cazaux *and* Rick Knowlton. 2017, $49.95 softcover (17.8 × 25.4 cm), 408pp., 71 illus., 297 diagrams, 9 maps, notes, bibliography, indexes, 978-0-7864-9427-9. The Persian and Arab game familiar for 500 years; similar games going back 1500 years still played; evolution of strategic board games especially in India, China and Japan; more recent chess variants (board sizes, new pieces, 3-D etc.). "Definitive" —IM John Donaldson; "impressive...one of the most interesting reads on the history of chess!"—*Chessbook Reviews*; "a wonderful and unique reference" —*Mind's Eye Press*.

Alexander Alekhine's Chess Games, 1902–1946. *2543 Games of the Former World Champion, Many Annotated by Alekhine, with 1868 Diagrams, Fully Indexed.*
Leonard M. Skinner *and* Robert G.P. Verhoeven. 2019 [original lib. bdg. 1998], $59.95 now softcover in 2 vols. (21.9 × 28.5 cm), 824pp., 1,868 diagrams, references, bibliography, indexes, 978-1-4766-7942-6. The most comprehensive accounting of the games. HISTORICAL BOOK OF THE YEAR—U.S. Chess Federation. FINALIST, BOOK OF THE YEAR—British Chess Federation.

José Raúl Capablanca. *A Chess Biography.*
Miguel A. Sánchez. 2015, $55 library binding (18.4 × 26 cm), 563pp., 195 annotated games, 55 illustrations, appendices, notes, bibliography, indexes, 978-0-7864-7004-4. "Amazing"—*Huffington Post;* "even the most ardent Capa fan will learn something new"—*Chess Life*; "a luxurious work and a true labor of love"—*Chess News*; "first rate...highly recommended"—IM John Donaldson.

Using the New In Chess app is easy!

- get early access to every issue
- replay all games in the Gameviewer

1

Sign in with your username and password to access the digital issue.

2

Read the article, optimized for your screen size.

3

Click on the Gameviewer button to get to the built-in chess board.

4

Replay the game, including an option to analyze with Stockfish.

The chess magazine that moves

www.newinchess.com/chess-apps

'Don't listen to other people's advice.'

CONTRIBUTORS TO THIS ISSUE
Erwin l'Ami, Jeroen Bosch, Maxim Dlugy, Daniil Dubov, Anish Giri, Wang Hao, John Henderson, Davorin Kuljasevic, Peter Heine Nielsen, Maxim Notkin, Judit Polgar, Jonathan Rowson, Matthew Sadler, Han Schut, Wesley So, Jan Timman

Golden Pawn
Awards
in Monaco

Monaco has a rich chess tradition that goes back to the legendary tournaments between 1901 and 1903 financed by the Georgian prince Dadiani. On November 30 a new chapter was opened with the inaugural European Golden Pawn Awards in the opulent Salle Empire of the Hotel de Paris next to the Monte Carlo casino. The event was organized by the European Chess Union and sponsored by the Georgian company AiGroup. According to ECU president Zurab Azmaiparashvili the Awards have been guaranteed for at least four years.

During a gala dinner, awards in twelve categories were presented, such as 'best European novel on chess', and awards honouring legendary players. New In Chess was chosen as best European chess magazine. At the end of the evening the winners posed for a group portrait: Frederic Friedel (ChessBase), Bessel Kok (chess organizer), Ruben David Gonzalez Gallego (novelist, with his sister Anna), Judit Polgar, Maya Chiburdanizde, Leontxo Garcia (journalist), Nona Gaprindashvili, Garry Kasparov, Geurt Gijssen (arbiter), Dirk Jan ten Geuzendam (New In Chess) and Alexander Kostyev (chess in schools).

O Captain! My Captain!

He invented the internationally recognized system of tri-coloured lights that made sailing at night less dangerous. Captain William Davies Evans also invented his eponymous gambit 1.e4 e5 2.♘f3 ♘c6 3.♗c4 ♗c5 4.b4 that equally could have used a similar warning system for unsuspecting opponents. The Captain's services to both maritime safety and chess were honoured recently with the unveiling of a a blue plaque tribute.

The ceremonial unveiling of the tribute to the inventor of the Evans Gambit.

Evans was born at Musland Farm in the Parish of St Dogwells in Wales on January 27, 1790. He had a fascination for both chess and the sea and in 1804 he enlisted in the Royal Navy to fight for King and Country, rising to the rank of captain. In the 1820s, he commanded a sailing packet that carried mail between Milford Haven and Waterford. And famously, on one such crossing, while leafing through the Giuoco Piano section in Sarratt's *New Treatise on the Game of Chess*, he had the brainwave of a new daring move that led to the birth of the Evans Gambit.

The sea-farer's swashbuckling gambit soon became popular and adopted by the likes of McDonnell, Labourdonnais, Anderssen, Morphy, Chigorin and Steinitz before it fell out of fashion for top players at the start of the 20th century – until Garry Kasparov dramatically rehabilitated Evans' old gambit by beating a very surprised Vishy Anand at the 1995 Tal Memorial in Riga.

The blue plaque monument was unveiled unveiled on 19 October by descendants of the Captain and affixed to a stone located on Wolfscastle village green. The stone was provided by Paul Evans of Musland Farm, where Captain Evans was born.

Ravens in London

Looking for a night at a London theatre with the lure of an intriguing new chess-themed psychological thriller? We doubt you will go far wrong with Tom Morton-Smith's *Ravens: Spassky vs. Fischer*, which runs November 29 to January 18 at the Hampstead Theatre, where already there's early chatter of a possible West End/Broadway production run.

The dramatization of the fabled Cold War chess face-off takes audiences back to the heady days of Reykjavik, 1972, when global media attention on the 'Match of the Century' sparked a proxy battle of differing political ideologies. It stars Ronan Raftery, whose screen work includes *Fresh Meat* and *Fantastic Beasts*, as Soviet World champion Boris Spassky, with his eventual nemesis, America's Bobby Fischer, played by *His Dark Materials* and *Chernobyl* actor Robert Emms.

Playwright Tom Morton-Smith (whose breakthrough drama was the critically-acclaimed *Oppenheimer* in 2015) was fascinated by the way huge global tensions were concentrated

Ronan Raftery and Robert Emms make you relive the 1972 Spassky-Fischer match.

during the Fischer-Spassky clash, and he's looking to reproduce that pressure-cooker environment onstage. 'There's this stand-off between these two superpowers and you find a little release valve in this chess match', he says. 'It was massive. For weeks it became front-page news. Chess had never been as big – and has never been as big since.'

Movie night

And if not the theatre, then how about a movie? Gérard Depardieu's new feel-good movie, *Fahim, the Little Chess Prince*, directed by acclaimed French filmmaker Pierre-François Martin-Laval, was released in Paris in mid-October to rave reviews and high ratings on IMDb.

The movie is based on the award-winning 2014 book of Fahim's story,

Time to resign for Gérard Depardieu in Fahim, the Little Chess Prince.

Le Roi Clandestin (the clandestine king), by children's author Sophie Le Callennec and Xavier Parmentier.

This is the inspiring true story of eight-year-old budding chess prodigy Fahim Mohammad. In 2008, Fahim and his father were forced to flee their native Bangladesh due to political persecution for the French capital. And, refused asylum in Paris, as illegal immigrants they soon spiral downwards into homelessness and desperation. But amidst all the emotional turmoil in his young life, Fahim has a life-changing experience after his chance meeting with one of France's top chess coaches, Parmentier (Depardieu's character, 'Sylvain

Charpentier), and the pair immediately strike up a connection.

Under his coach's tutelage, Fahim became the French U-12 champion. The following year he also won the World Schools Championship U-13 title – and this is what directly led to the family finding security and stability, as they were rewarded with French residency following his success.

Cryptic plans

We almost choked over our cornflakes when we read in a recent *Guardian* scoop that World Chess will now be using their very own unique brand of professional expertise to entice investors with plans to issue a cryptocurrency-like digital token ahead of a stock market float in London.

World Chess CEO and founder Ilya Merenzon said they are looking to raise 'low millions of euros' from the token offering. The tokens will use blockchain ledgers to simplify

Ilya Merenzon is looking for 'low millions of euros'.

the fundraising process, he adds, and these will be convertible to shares at a later point. Further cashing-in on the game, the company also announced they would be looking to develop a €25 ($27.50) per year online chess platform.

They say that a contract with FIDE means the platform will allow users to earn points in online games that could count towards an official FIDE world ranking and titles. All of this

was, er, news to FIDE, who immediately issued a statement clarifying a number of 'misleading facts'.

The first was that World Chess – which they emphasized was a private company, and separate from the governing body of the game – no longer organize, nor have the broadcasting rights to any future World Championship Match, Candidate Tournament etc. – they currently only run the Grand Prix 2019 and a similar series in 2021. FIDE also confirmed that they have no intention to use either the online platform or its titles and ratings for any official event before first conducting a thorough and detailed examination to ensure the 'proper functioning of the platform.'

Rock to Rook

We're always digging up stories about old chess pieces – and yet another has come to our attention via *Archaeology Magazine*, with news in their October issue that a Canadian archaeologist who found a carved rock in 1991 now believes it could be the world's oldest chess piece.

University of Victoria professor John Oleson says that the piece of carved sandstone that he found in southern Jordan at Humayma could well be an ancient rook. The roughly 1,300-year-old palm-sized stone is squat and rectangular, with 'horn-like projections'. Initially Oleson thought his find resembled other artefacts – but after re-examining it once again, and comparing the rock

The oldest chess piece ever? A rook?

carving to other early chess pieces, he thought the parallels were 'far more convincing.'

'Since the Humayma object was found in a seventh-century context, it would be the earliest known physical example for the simplified, abstract design,' said Oleson, 'and possibly the earliest known example of a chess piece altogether.'

The Laws of Chess

Honest, nothing to do with the FIDE Rules Committee. This is, believe it or not, about a US legal book that makes a distinct comparison between law and chess. In the

The marriage of chess and law must make for a page-turner.

new hefty tome, *Chess and the Law: An Anthology of Anecdotes and Analogies*, law clerk and attorney Andrew J. Field takes us on a journey documenting the intersection of the game of chess and the law.

According to the blurb: 'Chess and the Law is filled with true crime, chess history, and legal history. It is also a valuable desk reference for judges and attorneys in search of elegant chess quotes for their legal writing. *Chess and the Law* is many things, blended together in a book that quickly transforms from anthology to page-turner.'

It even featured in the October *New York Law Journal*, with one reviewer noting that: 'Field's book (..) is creative, it is wise, it is funny, it is philosophical, and it is easy to read.' ∎

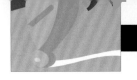
Decades apart

Being a child of a grandmaster, I remember New In Chess fondly as a part of my formative years, both with regards to getting to know the magical world chess, as well as the English language. In fact, even today, I read it with the utmost interest and it never fails to deliver.

After reading, in New In Chess 2019/6, the reporting on Michael Adams' great victory in the British Championship, decades apart from his first win, I noticed that you asked if any readers knew about similar feats. I am glad to chip in here: My father, GM Johann Hjartarson, became the Icelandic Champion in 1980 (at the age of 17) and 2016 (when he was 53). That makes it 36 years in between, if the arithmetic doesn't fail me. He collected 4 additional titles within this period, in 1984, 1994, 1995 and 1997.

My father was a professional chess player for many years and quit in 1998. Today he plays only for fun. Since we are on the topic, I might add that he became Nordic champion in 1997 and again in 2017, without ever taking part in between.

Hjörtur Ingvi Jóhannsson,
Garðabær, Iceland

A mystery

With some sadness, I shall not be renewing my subscription this time. The reason lies with me, not with the magazine (which continues to be very high quality). About five years ago, and quite inexplicably, my enthusiasm for chess simply disappeared, as if a light switch had been turned off in my mind. I no longer had any interest in playing, and I very rarely read my chess books and magazines. My efforts to re-ignite my former feelings for the game have failed.

It is all a mystery to me. I have loved chess since my school days. In the first chess magazine I ever owned, I remember being gripped by reports of the tense hostilities in the Kortchnoi-Petrosian Candidates match in 1977. My first contact with New In Chess was like striking gold: I received a sample copy, which turned out to be the issue with Tony Miles's amazing account of his experiences at the Tilburg tournament in 1985. What a fabulous introduction to your magazine! Since then, I have acquired and enjoyed almost a complete run from the very start.

After more than three decades, therefore, it is time to say Goodbye and – more importantly – Thank You to everyone at New In Chess, past and present, for so many years of stimulating reading.

Andrew Farthing
Brockhill Village, Norton, Worcester, UK

Cheap exaggeration

I was surprised in New In Chess 2019/7 to see Sasha Chapin's *All The Wrong Moves* eulogised, among other things, for its author's 'keen, spot-on observations on chess', and the way he 'avoids ... cheap exaggerations'.

Really? The book begins with a preface entitled 'The 600 Million', because Chapin is happy to believe and repeat that made-up figure for the number of chess players there are in the world. To use his own phrase, it's 'objectively nonsensical' – if it were anywhere close to true, we would be seeing chess and chess players everywhere, much as we do football and footballers, and yet practically the opposite is the truth.

Only a moment should be required to ask oneself whether that figure can possibly be accurate, and another few moments to find, from the internet, that it is very much a 'cheap exaggeration' and has been comprehensively debunked. This, however, seems to have been beyond Mr Chapin, and therefore taking him at all seriously as a chess writer is beyond this particular reader.

Justin Horton
Huesca, Spain

Editorial postscript:

You are right, the claim that there are 600 million chess players in the world is 'objectively nonsensical' and has been debunked several times in this magazine as well. In fact, I had made a note to mention it in my review, but I forgot, possibly because there is such an abundance of great chess writing in the rest of the book (DJtG).

Reducing draws and longevity

I am writing about two unrelated topics in New In Chess 2019/6. First, on the proposal to count only victories in order to reduce draws. While it would undoubtedly do so, the victories would have no meaning if the opponents had no reward for trying to save draws in inferior positions.

Faster time limits and/or switching to Chess 960 will also reduce draws, but of course there are drawbacks to these solutions. My preferred solution is to award more than half a point (maybe 0.6 or 0.7) for giving stalemate and for reaching King and

minor piece vs. King (which could only be claimed when the side with the minor is on move). I don't know if FIDE would rate such an event, but they already rate many events that give both players only 1/3 of the point (1 out of 3 points, same thing) for any draw, which I consider far more radical and disruptive than my proposal.

On the topic of longevity in master chess and Sarapu's record span of 38 years between national championships, I can't challenge that record without some 'cheating', but if we allow national open championships and World (Senior) championships, then I can claim a span of 42 years from winning the American Open Championship in 1966 (ahead of the late, great GM Pal Benko) to winning the World Senior in 2008 (with 14 GMs participating).

If we allow ties for championships lost on tiebreak, then it's 44 years as I also tied for the World Senior in 2010 but placed 4th on tiebreak. And regarding State Championships, my span is 45 years for the nine Maryland championships I won from 1971 to 2016. I realize that 'state' is not a term used everywhere in the world, so I would say that any regional championship of a defined area with at least a million people should count. I imagine that others have beaten my record, perhaps

readers can identify the record-holder. Actually by this definition I can claim 50 years from the 1966 American Open to the 2016 Md. Open. That might be a record!?

(Addendum: I forgot that while I was a student at M.I.T., I won the Massachusetts Championship in 1965 and 1968, so my total span for state championships is 51 years, 1965 to 2016.)

GM Larry Kaufman
Bethesda, MD, USA

Open is not closed

I just received New In Chess 2019/7 and turned to Jan Timman's tribute to Pal Benko. In the heading '8-Time US Champion' is a serious error. Please insert 'Open' after 'US.' These are vastly different tournaments in format and strength. Pal Benko was never tops in the US (Closed) Championship and sometimes even finished as low as I did.

Anthony Saidy
Hollywood, United States

COLOPHON

PUBLISHER: Allard Hoogland
EDITOR-IN-CHIEF:
Dirk Jan ten Geuzendam
HONORARY EDITOR: Jan Timman
CONTRIBUTING EDITOR: Anish Giri
EDITORS: Peter Boel, René Olthof
PRODUCTION: Joop de Groot
TRANSLATORS: Ken Neat, Piet Verhagen
SALES AND ADVERTISING: Remmelt Otten

PHOTOS AND ILLUSTRATIONS IN THIS ISSUE:
Maria Emelianova, Valeria Gordienko,
Mark Livshits, Lennart Ootes, Berend Vonk

COVER PHOTO: Lennart Ootes

© No part of this magazine may be reproduced, stored in a retrieval system or transmitted in any form or by any means, recording or otherwise, without the prior permission of the publisher.

NEW IN CHESS
P.O. BOX 1093
1810 KB ALKMAAR
THE NETHERLANDS

PHONE: 00-31-(0)72-51 27 137
SUBSCRIPTIONS: nic@newinchess.com
EDITORS: editors@newinchess.com
ADVERTISING: otten@newinchess.com

WWW.NEWINCHESS.COM

The exciting impact of a game changer
When Magnus met AlphaZero

Magnus Carlsen and Peter Heine Nielsen at the St. Louis Chess Club. It's been a great year for the World Champion and the head of his analytical team, not in the last place thanks to the inspiration of AlphaZero.

AlphaZero's play has sent shockwaves through the chess world. Magnus Carlsen even confessed that he has become a different player thanks to the inspiration of the revolutionary engine (and Daniil Dubov). **PETER HEINE NIELSEN** looks back on a wonderful year for the World Champion and the role AlphaZero played in his successes.

Imagine a spaceship landing in the centre of London, friendly aliens having a quick look at the tourist attractions and then quietly leaving again. Apart from the initial shock, I assume life would resume its normal course, except for the fact that we would seriously have to question our technological level and anyone in power would probably be paranoid about the 'aliens' teaming up with their enemies.

For chess players, that is how it felt in December 2017, when DeepMind released 10 of the games from the match in which its creation AlphaZero utterly crushed Stockfish, the strongest available engine, in a 100-game match. The London Chess Classic was under way at the time, and we continued preparing for and analysing the games with Stockfish. What else could we do?

At the closing dinner, Demis Hassabis, a former chess prodigy who is now CEO of DeepMind, held a Q&A session in which he explained that AlphaZero was part of the company's scientific research (in the meantime they have shifted their attention to real-world problems and are playing Starcraft). They had no intentions of upsetting the chess world, but were (justifiably) proud of breathing new life in the attacking prospects in chess.

Long-term initiative

The ten games that they published certainly achieved this. One was even more beautiful than the next, with AlphaZero giving up pawns and even pieces for a long-term initiative. Most chess experts would have considered this impossible to do against Stockfish until we actually saw it happen. DeepMind also published an academic paper in which they explained the premises of their research. Hungry for every bit of

information, curious chess players obviously read the smallest details, looking to extract as much knowledge as they could.

The following formula:

$$(\mathbf{p}, v) = f_\theta(s), \quad l = (z - v)^2 - \boldsymbol{\pi}^\top \log \mathbf{p} + c\|\theta\|^2$$

is explained at great length, but I think it left us just as wise as non-chess players reading chess notation.

Still, apart from the ten games, the paper did have quite some chess info. Besides playing the main match, DeepMind took the twelve most common opening complexes from human games, and held separate 100 games matches with these as well.

As we could see in a graph, Alpha-Zero scored 27 wins in 50 games as White in the main line of the Spanish – an amazing feat, considering that it was World Champion Magnus Carlsen's main opening at the time and that no-one, not even Sergey Karjakin in the 2016 World Championship match, had come

close to setting him any theoretical problems.

The moves given in the graph are AlphaZero's preferred choices for both colours, but brutally stop after 7.♗b3 0-0. We still don't know if AlphaZero prefers the topical 8.a4!? or whether it has actually refuted the Marshall Gambit and plays 8.c3, but that just like Fermat and his famous theorem they thought there was not enough space in the margins to actually inform us.

200 new games!

A year passed, and then DeepMind published another paper, this time with 200 new games! They even politely waited for the 2018 World

Championship match between Magnus and Fabiano Caruana to finish before publishing the paper, not risking that some novelty played by AlphaZero would influence the match.

Again they were beautiful games, interesting novelties and explanations of AlphaZero's 'thought-processes' in one of its most impressive wins.

But we were still basically left to do our own interpretation of how AlphaZero had renewed chess until, in January 2019, the book *Game Changer* was published, which was literally a game changer! The authors Natasha Regan and Matthew Sadler had had exclusive access to the DeepMind team behind AlphaZero, and to a far larger number of games than had been published.

They had asked for experiments to be done, as well as created hypotheses on why AlphaZero plays like it does,

getting help from the team to either confirm or refute these thoughts. All this is clearly presented in an academic style in *Game Changer*. The book was fittingly presented during the Wijk aan Zee tournament in the Netherlands, where the world elite was gathered, so everybody could start reading and deepening their understanding of chess, and then apply their own interpretation of the new knowledge in the upcoming tournaments.

As Magnus Carlsen stated during a press-conference in Stavanger during this year's Norway Chess tournament in June: 'In essence I have become a very different player in terms of style than I was a bit earlier, and it has

One game was even more beautiful than the next, with AlphaZero giving up pawns and even pieces for a long-term initiative.

Magnus Carlsen: 'In essence I have become a very different player in terms of style than I was a bit earlier, and it has been a great ride.'

been a great ride', acknowledging the inspiration from AlphaZero, and Daniil Dubov!

Pushing the h-pawn

In Shamkir, at the Vugar Gashimov Memorial, Magnus successfully sacrificed pawns, and in Norway Chess we saw a couple of examples of him successfully following the AlphaZero concept of aggressively pushing his h-pawn towards his opponent's king.

Game Changer devotes a full chapter to this concept. Here's what Magnus did in Stavanger.

Magnus Carlsen
Shakhriyar Mamedyarov
Stavanger 2019
Grünfeld Defence, Exchange Variation

1.d4 ♘f6 2.c4 g6 3.♘c3 d5 4.cxd5 ♘xd5 5.e4 ♘xc3 6.bxc3 ♗g7 7.♗e3

AlphaZero's favourite against the Grünfeld, which we knew already from the 2017 paper. But with no further moves or explanations! None of the original test games vs. Stockfish featured the Grünfeld, since Stockfish does not play it as Black unless forced to. So, for the sake of the experiment in connection with the writing of *Game Changer*, test games were played, with the position after 2...

g6 3.♘c3 being mandatory, which resulted in 3...d5 4.cxd5 ♘xd5 5.♘f3 ♗g7 6.e4 ♘xc3 7.bxc3 c5 8.♗e3 ♕a5 9.♕d2 ♘c6 10.♖b1 a6 11.♖c1 cxd4 12.cxd4 ♕xd2+ 13.♔xd2 e6 14.♗d3 ♗d7 15.e5 0-0 16.♖b1 b5 17.h4 ♘e7 18.h5 ♗c6 19.h6!.

This led to a beautiful win and a model game of utilizing the h-pawn to cramp Black's king's position even in a queenless middlegame!
7...c5 8.♖c1 0-0 9.♘f3

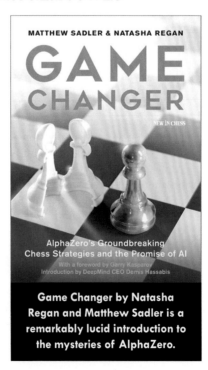

MATTHEW SADLER & NATASHA REGAN

GAME CHANGER

NEW IN CHESS

AlphaZero's Groundbreaking
Chess Strategies and the Promise of AI

With a foreword by Garry Kasparov
Introduction by DeepMind CEO Demis Hassabis

Game Changer by Natasha Regan and Matthew Sadler is a remarkably lucid introduction to the mysteries of AlphaZero.

9...♘d7

After 9...♕a5 10.♕d2 ♗g4 11.d5 b5 12.♗e2 ♘d7 13.0-0 ♗xf3 14.♗xf3 c4 15.♗e2 ♖fd8 16.f4 ♘b6 17.♗f3 ♕a3 18.h4 Magnus went on to beat Grischuk earlier on in the same tournament (for my further notes see New In Chess 2019/5, pp.21-24).
10.♗e2 ♕a5 11.0-0 ♕xa2 12.♘d2 ♕a5 13.h4 b5 14.h5 ♗b7 15.h6 ♗h8 16.e5

As this game was already debated in detail in New In Chess 2019/5 (pp. 20-21), I will not rehash the comments, but this is a text-book example of the AlphaZero attacking concept. Black's king is crowded by the bishop on h8, and an attempt to liberate the position with ...f6 often will be met by a deadly check on the a2-g8 diagonal, at times even at the cost of material. It is true that the bishop on h8 does parry mating threats on g7, preventing White's most basic kind of attack, but a slower, much more irresistible wave is coming, starting with f4 next.

In short: Black could be a pawn up, with no immediate white threats, yet strategically he is lost! (Although Mamedyarov managed to escape with a draw after 46 moves.)

In his game against Magnus Carlsen at Norway Chess, Shakhriyar Mamedyarov
was not ready yet to take the march of the h-pawn one step further.

Not ready yet

Interestingly, these same players
could have been in a similar situation
two months earlier in Shamkir, but at
that point the 'march of the h-pawn'
had not caught on yet.

Magnus Carlsen
Shakhriyar Mamedyarov
Shamkir 2019

position after 20.♘c5

When you think about this game
from the Gashimov Memorial earlier
in the year, this position springs to
mind. Mamedyarov continued in
traditional fashion, stepping up the
pressure along the h-file, and it was

only very accurate defending that
allowed Magnus to keep the balance.
The game ended in a draw after:
**20...♔g7 21.♗xb4 axb4 22.♖xa8
♖xa8 23.♖a1 ♖h8 24.♕e1
hxg3 25.hxg3 ♘e4 26.♘xe4
♗xe4 27.♗xe4 dxe4 28.♖a5
♖h5 29.♖xh5 gxh5 30.♔g2 c5
31.dxc5 ♕xc5 32.♕d1 ♕c3
33.♕d5 ♔f6 34.♕d6+ ♔g7
35.♕d5 ♔f6 36.♕d6+ ♔g7
37.♕d5 ♔f6** Draw.

No one seemed to contest that this
was the logical turn of events; neither
the live commentary nor the press
conference that followed paid any
attention to this position.
Maybe humanity is just not ready for
it yet, but it seems likely that in the
diagrammed position, AlphaZero
would have played 20...h3!?. At first,
Stockfish laughs at this move, but
then it goes along and evaluates it
as 0.00, like quite some other moves
in the position. After 21.♗h1 ♕e7
22.♖ca1 White does break through
on the queenside, but 22...♗xc5
23.dxc5 ♘e4

gives counterplay, the principal
point being that 24.♖xa5? ♖xa5
25.♖xa5 d4! wins instantly for Black,
as White's position cannot defend
against the immediate threats. Even
more cunning might be 23...♗e4!?,
when after 24.f3 ♗d3 25.♖xa5 ♖xa5
26.♖xa5 ♘d7

Black has excellent compensation. The bishop will relocate to b5,
combining the defence of c6 and
control of the squares around White's
king, while Black's knight will aim
for d3, or if 27.b4 ♘e5, possibly also
c4. True, White does have an extra
pawn, but we are playing for much
higher stakes.
21.♗h1 may be just wrong. If the
bishop ends up stuck on h1 with a
pawn on f3, then it just crowds the
white king, depriving it of an escape
square. This makes 21.♗f3 a logical
move, but then Black can start
aiming at the bishop by transfer-
ring a knight to g5. If it retreats to e2
then, after a ...♗xc5 scenario, ...♕e4
will threaten mate on g2. Black starts
with 21...♕e7, with a very interesting
struggle ahead.

King mobility

In *Game Changer* the authors make the highly interesting statistical observation that AlphaZero seems to value 'king mobility' a lot more highly than traditional engines. Obviously, this will manifest itself in the later stage of the games, since AlphaZero wins more often than it loses, and a game of chess is decided by giving checkmate, the ultimate removal of all mobility from the opponent's king!

15...♘c6 16.♘f3 ♘e7 17.♘e5 ♘g6 18.f4 ♘xe5 19.fxe5 ♗c6, when Black manages to threaten mate on g2 just in time before White plays ♖f3, and after 20.g3 ♖d7 Black's resources have proved sufficient to hold the balance. Strangely enough, White's 'safe' king becomes the problem, because Black uses it to win an important tempo when reorganizing his defence. At the same time, the possibilities to attack Black's king are restricted, since White cannot

> **A game of chess is decided by giving checkmate, the ultimate removal of all mobility from the opponent's king!**

But in the opening stages of the game, the statistics also show that AlphaZero prefers to have more squares available around its king for it to feel comfortable.

Magnus Carlsen
Levon Aronian
Zagreb 2019
Queen's Gambit Declined, Vienna Variation

1.d4 ♘f6 2.c4 e6 3.♘f3 d5 4.♘c3 ♗b4 5.♗g5 dxc4 6.e4 c5 7.e5 cxd4 8.♘xd4 ♗xc3+ 9.bxc3 ♕a5 10.exf6 ♕xg5 11.fxg7 ♕xg7 12.♕d2 0-0 13.♗xc4 ♖d8 14.♕e3 ♗d7

Before this game White had always castled kingside, 15.0-0, in this position. It is the obvious move, safeguarding the king before further action, with games continuing

attack freely on the kingside when his own king is located there. So Magnus played:

15.0-0-0

A spectacular move, at least by our traditional understanding of chess. But AlphaZero might approve! While Black's king is restricted on g8, White's on c1 has a lot more mobility – in a strict mathematical sense 4 vs 2 available squares. Of course, White's king is not 'safe' by traditional standards, but is it less safe than Black's counterpart on g8? If White castles short, positional features where White's pawn on c3 looks weak become a factor, while with opposite castling the relative king safety becomes the relevant factor. And White has the easier plan, aiming for h4 and ♖h3. Like with the h6/...h3 positions, it would be a bold statement to say that 15.0-0-0 is a better plan than the traditional ones, but it is interesting and has every right to exist, and leads to a far more complex battle!

15...♘c6 16.♗b3 ♗e8

16...♕e5 has been seen in similar positions, with Black trying to temper White's attack by exchanging queens, but after 17.♕h6 ♕g7 White will not repeat but retreat to either h5 or h4.

17.♘xc6 ♗xc6 18.h4 ♕f6
19.♖h3

19...b5

Here Magnus uses another theme
from *Game Changer*, the rook lift, zig-
zagging his rook to the proximity of
Black's king. But maybe it would have
been better to 'go full AlphaZero'
on Black: 20.h5!? b4 21.h6!, and
things are anything but simple for
Black after 21...♕xc3+ 22.♕xc3 bxc3
23.♖xd8+ ♖xd8 24.♖xc3, since the
rook ending after 24...♗d5 25.♗xd5
exd5 26.♖c6, followed by a4, is close
to being lost. But since 21...♔h8
22.g4!, threatening 23.g5, only makes
things worse for Black, his position is
hard to defend.
**20.♖g3+ ♔h8 21.♖g4 a5 22.♖f4
♕g7 23.♖xd8+ ♖xd8 24.g4 b4
25.g5 bxc3 26.♗c2 ♗d5 27.♖f6**

27...♕f8!

Aronian manages to create counter-
threats just in time, and defended
brilliantly to save the game.
**28.♕xc3 ♖c8! 29.♕d3 ♕g7
30.f4 ♔g8 31.♔d2 h6 32.a3
hxg5 33.fxg5 ♖c4 34.♕g3 ♗e4
35.♗b3 ♖d4+ 36.♔e1 ♗f5 37.h5**

♖d3 38.♕b8+ ♕f8 39.♕xf8+
♔xf8 40.♗c2 ♖h3 41.♗xf5 exf5
42.h6 ♔g8 43.a4 ♖h4 44.♖xf5
♖xa4 45.♔f2 ♖g4 46.♔f3 ♖g1
47.♔f2 ♖g4 48.♔f3 ♖g1 49.♔f2
Draw.

A few months later, the world's two
highest-rated humans butted heads
in Isle of Man, and again Magnus
chose a spectacular way to castle.

Magnus Carlsen
Fabiano Caruana
Douglas 2019 (9)

position after 10...0-0

Here Magnus played: **11.0-0-0!?**
The similarity to the Aronian game
is striking. White again castles into
open space, but this time Black even
has a 'perfect' castle, with pawns at f7,
g7 and h7. The *Game Changer* king-
mobility count, however, is a 4-1 in
favour of White. More importantly,
Black's kingside is unprotected, especially with the bishop as far away as
on a5. As in the Aronian game, the
weakness of the c-pawn(s) becomes
less important with opposite castling.
The question now is who gets to the
opposite king first?
    For the rest of this game I refer to
Erwin l'Ami's notes in his report on
the Isle of Man Grand Swiss else-
where in this issue.

Turning things upside down
Apart from general concepts, *Game
Changer* also debates a number of
AlphaZero's specific opening ideas,
and analyses them in great detail.
This has not gone unnoticed either.

Wesley So
Magnus Carlsen
Stavanger (Armageddon) 2019
Anti-Grünfeld Indian
**1.d4 ♘f6 2.c4 g6 3.f3 d5 4.cxd5
♘xd5 5.e4 ♘b6 6.♘c3 ♗g7 7.♗e3
0-0 8.♕d2 ♘c6 9.0-0-0 f5 10.e5 f4**

An amazing concept. After 10.e5 Black
usually continued 10...♘b4, when after
11.♘h3 White kept a positional bind
that at times turned into a kingside
attack (with Magnus' own spectacular
win against Li Chao, Doha 2015, as the
primary example).
With 10...f4!? AlphaZero turned things
upside down, sacrificing a pawn, saying
that with opposite castling, mobility
and time are more important. In *Game
Changer* they analyse: 11.♗xf4 ♘b4
12.h4 ♗e6 13.h5 c5 14.hxg6 ♕c7!! 15.
gxh7+ ♔h8 16.♗h6 cxd4 17.♗xg7+
♔xg7 18.♕h6+ ♔h8 19.♖xd4 ♘xa2+
20.♔d2 ♕e5 21.♕e3

So why did AlphaZero play it? Simply
because it found it was Black's relatively
best option! This was a training game
with the position till 9...f5 being forced
and AlphaZero saying 'I strongly object
to this position, but having said that,
how about this pawn sacrifice?'

11.♗f2 ♘b4 As this was a blitz game, the following moves indeed lack accuracy, but in the end Magnus exploits the mobility created by 10...f4!?, but then agrees to repetition, as this was an Armageddon game.

12.a3 a5 13.h4 ♗e6 14.♘h3 ♘a2+ 15.♘xa2 ♗xa2 16.d5 ♕xd5 17.♕xd5+ ♘xd5 18.♖e1 ♖f5 19.♗d3 ♖xe5 20.♖xe5 ♗xe5 21.h5 gxh5 22.♘g5 ♘f6

23.♘xh7 ♖d8 24.♗c2 ♗f7 25.♘g5 ♗d4 26.♗e1 b6 27.♗h4 ♗e3+ 28.♔b1 ♖d2 29.♘xf7 ♔xf7 30.♗xf6 ♔xf6 31.♖xh5 ♖xg2

32.♖h6+ ♔e5 33.♖h5+ ♔d6 34.♖h6+ ♔e5 35.♖h5+ ♔d6 36.♖h6+ Draw.

In their Armageddon game at Norway Chess, Magnus Carlsen defeated Wesley So with an amazing concept that AlphaZero had found in a training game.

The absolutely sharpest choice

In what is maybe the sharpest of all openings, the Anti-Moscow Gambit, AlphaZero also had its say, adding to a debate that is very much on the opening theorists' radar.

Magnus Carlsen
Maxim Matlakov
Douglas 2019 (10)
Semi-Slav, Anti-Moscow Gambit

1.♘f3 ♘f6 2.d4 d5 3.c4 e6 4.♘c3 c6 5.♗g5 h6 6.♗h4

AlphaZero goes for the absolutely sharpest choice, the Anti-Moscow Gambit, in which White sacrifices a full pawn for long-term compensation. We tend to describe AlphaZero's style as aggressive, with a strong willingness to give up material for the initiative. This view was very much influenced by the first 10 published games of 2017, but still holds when you see the 2018 games. Yet how does that explain its preference for the Berlin as Black? It is hard to see any other reason than that the Berlin is a good or even optimal choice! No matter whether efficiency means sacrificing material or being incredibly solid, they will do what is required! Regardless of whether they are the pinnacle of AI or the Chess World Champion.

6...dxc4 7.e4 g5 8.♗g3 b5 9.h4

> No matter whether efficiency means sacrificing material or being incredibly solid, they will do what is required! Regardless of whether they are the pinnacle of AI or the Chess World Champion.

At the FIDE Grand Swiss, Magnus Carlsen created a strategic gem against Maxim Matlakov with an idea gleaned from a game between AlphaZero and Stockfish.

I seconded Vishy Anand in the 2007 World Championship in Mexico, where the Anti-Moscow Gambit was all the rage. In those days, however, White would either push h4 a bit later or not at all. AlphaZero adds its own flavour:

9...g4 10.♘e5 ♘bd7 11.♗e2

11...♗b7

In the AlphaZero-Stockfish game a different move-order appeared: 11...♘xe5 12.♗xe5 ♖g8 13.0-0 ♗b7 14.♖e1 a6 15.g3. What was striking in this AlphaZero game was the absolute calmness in the style of play, believing that the long-term compensation is sufficient and thus calmly improving the position as if there is absolutely no hurry at all to prove that White's initiative compensates for the investment: 15...h5 16.♕c2 ♘d7 17.♗f4 ♖g6 18.b3 b4 19.♘a4 c3

Black gets a protected passed pawn, but that doesn't seem to worry AlphaZero the slightest either, since it instead gets access to the b1-h7 diagonal for its bishop and can continue to slowly improve its

position: 20.e5 ♕c7 21.♗d3 ♖g8 22.♗h7 ♖h8 23.♗e4 a5 24.a3 ♗e7 25.♗g2 ♖d8 26.axb4 axb4 27.♕e4 ♖b8 28.♖ed1!.

ANALYSIS DIAGRAM

A strategic gem has materialized. Black is basically committed to passively waiting for White to try to break through, as 28...c5 will now be met strongly by 29.d5 ♗xd5 30.♖xd5 exd5 31.♕xd5, when the exchange sac turns White's long-term prospects into an immediate tactical win. 28...♖d8 29.♔h2 ♖a8 30.♗e3 ♘b6 31.♘xb6 ♖xa1 32.♖xa1 ♕xb6 33.♕f4 ♕c7 34.♗e4 ♕d8

ANALYSIS DIAGRAM

35.f3!. Breaking Black's 'fortress'. 35...♖g8 36.♕h6 ♔d7 37.♕xh5 ♕e8 38.♕h6 ♕b8 39.♕f4 f5 40.exf6 ♕xf4 41.♗xf4 ♗xf6 42.fxg4 ♗c8 43.♖a4 ♗xh4 44.♖xb4 ♗f6 45.♖c4 ♔d8 46.♖xc3 ♖xg4 47.♖c4 ♖g7 48.♗xc6 ♗a6 49.♖b4 ♗c8 50.♔g2 ♖a7 51.♔f3 ♔e7 52.♗e5 ♗xe5 53.dxe5 ♖c7 54.♗e4 ♖c3+ 55.♔f4 ♖c1 56.♖c4 ♖f1+ 57.♔g5 1-0.

12.♘xd7 ♕xd7 13.♗e5 ♕e7

Had Matlakov retreated to d8, then after 13...♕d8 14.0-0 ♖g8 it would

Magnus' play is like that in the original ten AlphaZero games, with the initiative being a more important factor than the number of pawns

have been a straight transposition to the AlphaZero game!

14.b3!? Magnus immediately pokes the queenside, inviting Black to get his protected passed pawn on c3.

14...Zg8

Matlakov's idea is that 15.bxc4 b4 now allows Black to play 16...Dxe4, trading his queenside pawn for a central pawn. That would also lead to interesting complications, but Magnus stays loyal to the AlphaZero concept and protects his e4-pawn.

15.Wc2 b4 16.Da4 c3 17.a3

The inclusion of a3/...a5 generally favours White, not only because of the option of opening the a-file, but also because it gives access to the b6-square. Since 17...a5? 18.Db6! is very good for White, Matlakov has to make a couple of intermediate moves before protecting the b4-pawn.

17...Dd7 18.Bg3 Bg7 19.Zd1

A necessary precaution. 19.e5 c5! would be grim for White, because his centre would crumble.

19...a5 20.0-0

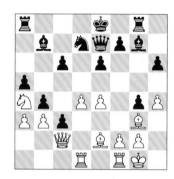

20...Bf6!? 20...e5 21.Bxg4 Zd8!? would also be interesting, trying to undermine the white centre and hoping to withstand the attacking possibilities White would get in the process. But Matlakov's move is obviously critical, trying to simply pick up the h4-pawn, and thus forcing Magnus to show his hand.

21.Dc5?!

The right plan, but the wrong execution! White indeed has to give up more pawns, but the incredible 21.Bc7!! was the way, when 21...Bxh4 22.e5 gives White a huge initiative for the two sacrificed pawns. 21...Zc8 would be logical, but the a3/...a5 inclusion means that 22.Bxa5! is possible!

21...Dxc5 22.dxc5 e5 23.Zd6

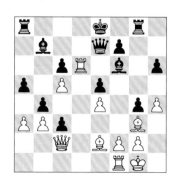

Magnus' play is like that in the original ten AlphaZero games, with the initiative being a more important factor than the number of pawns, even if objectively speaking Black is fine. But because he was short of time, Matlakov was facing a difficult practical job.

23...Bxh4 24.Bc4 Bg5 25.Wd3 Zg6 26.f4

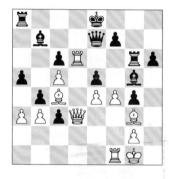

26...exf4? This logical move ruins Black's position. 26...gxf3 27.Wxf3 Zg7 will hold, but only if Black finds 28.Bxe5 Wxe5 29.Bxf7+ Kf8!? 30.Bc4+ Bf4!, when Black's passed pawn on c3 will finally show its relevance in the ensuing endgame.

27.Bxf4? In the post-game press conference Magnus said he had actually intended the crushing 27.e5!, but then somehow forgot!

27...Bxf4 28.Zxf4 c2 29.Wxc2 Zxd6 30.cxd6 Wxd6 31.e5! Wc5+ 32.Kh1 We3 33.Wf5

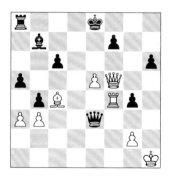

Black's king is caught in the centre, and although Magnus could have won more quickly, the result never was in doubt (1-0, 80). ■

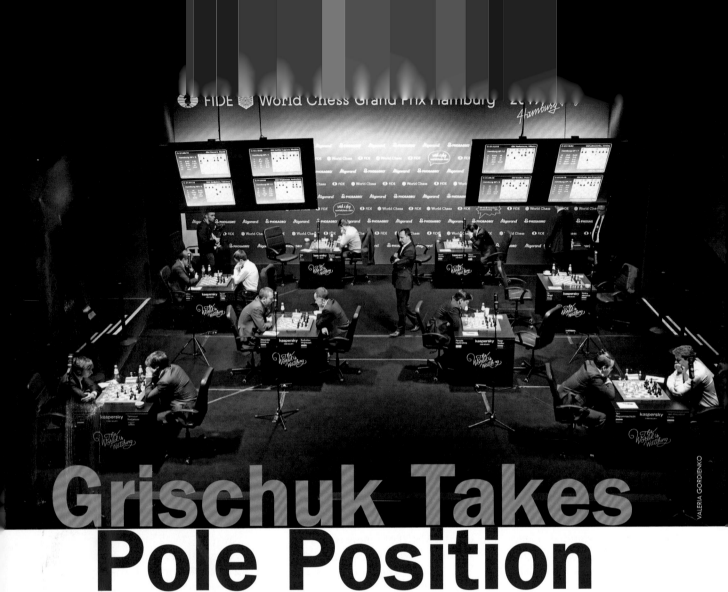

Grischuk Takes Pole Position

Russian looks set to play in Candidates again

By beating Jan-Krzysztof Duda in the final, Alexander Grischuk took first place in the Hamburg GP. The Russian also took the lead in the overall standings of the FIDE Grand Prix. Although he will not play in the final leg, in Jerusalem in December, Grischuk has excellent chances to claim one of the two spots in the Candidates Tournament that are at stake. **JOHN HENDERSON** reports.

T he penultimate leg of the FIDE Grand Prix in Hamburg produced a popular steely-eyed victor, Alexander Grischuk from Russia. In the tiebreak decider in the final the Muscovite got the better of Polish rising wannabe Jan-Krzysztof Duda. On the way to the final Grischuk had shaken off Radoslaw Wojtaszek, David Navara and one of his closest rivals for the desired spot in the Candidates, Maxime Vachier-Lagrave. The Candidates Tournament will be held in Yekaterinburg, Russia, next March.

The winner took the first prize of 24,000 euros and more crucially gained a further 10 GP points (eight for the victory and two bonus points for winning two matches without need of a tiebreak decider) and now tops the overall standings with 20 points. Vachier-Lagrave is in second place on 13 points, followed by Mamedyarov with 10 points, and Nepomniachtchi now trailing on 9 points.

Having played his 'cycle' of three nominated legs, Grischuk's Grand Prix is over. 'Now it will be very pleasant for me to watch the final event', wryly commented Grischuk in victory. 'Of course, I wish luck to everyone who can still qualify, to 'Shakh' Mamedyarov, to Nepomniachtchi and Maxime. But not too much luck to Maxime because I don't want him to overtake me. I cannot be rooting against myself!'

Mr. Golden Standard

For early GP front-runner Ian Nepomniachtchi (who won the Moscow leg), the frayed nerves were on show right from the off in

Opinions about the venue differed, but everyone agreed that the number of spectators was disappointing.

Hamburg. He suffered what proved to be a traumatic and inexplicable opening game loss to Duda that led to his early exit and ultimately could prove to be costly for the Russian. It then got worse, as he clashed on social media with the organizers.

Clearly frustrated, Nepomniachtchi tweeted that the organizers '... chose the most expensive and nice hotel and the most cheap and unsuitable playing venue. At least I rejoice I shouldn't go there anymore.' The spat only intensified with him further claiming that World Chess CEO Ilya Merenzon was 'Mr. Golden Standard of pathetic organization.' So no love lost there then, eh?

The current Grand Prix cycle indeed seems to be the swan-song for Merenzon's oft-criticized World Chess, with the new FIDE administration having dispensed with their 'invaluable expertise and services.'

(World Chess has lost the right to organize the World Championship, but still has the rights to organize the 2021 Grand Prix 'or a similar series' -ed.) Certainly the venue for the Hamburg Grand Prix left a lot to be desired, but most puzzling of all is that, with Germany being famous for big turnouts for any chess event, something certainly went wrong organization-wise. Clearly, there was no atmosphere being generated due to the sparsity of spectators, as we could all witness from the many empty chairs in the playing hall and also in the live commentary room.

Then again, Nepomniachtchi was probably looking to kick something after his horrific early exit to Duda, and the organizers – rightly or wrongly – were as good a candidate as any. Mind you, if there was any kicking needing to be done on Nepomniachtchi's part, then it was surely all self-inflicted over the board!

Jan-Krzysztof Duda
Ian Nepomniachtchi
Hamburg 2019 (1.1)

position after 23.♖d2

It is hard to be critical when there's so much pressure on the players vying for a Candidates spot, but here Nepo has what can only be best described in a family magazine as a 'brain freeze' with... **23...e4?** ... that not only blunders away a pawn but also, more crucially, the position, forgetting that he can't recapture on e4 due to the little matter of the mate on g7! And with it, his position goes downhill rapidly.

Nepomniachtchi tweeted that the organizers '...chose the most expensive and nice hotel and the most cheap and unsuitable playing venue.'

Ian Nepomniachtchi vented his frustration about his early elimination in a derogatory tweet about the organization.

24.♗xe4 ♖d7 25.♗f5 ♖d5 26.e4

26...♖xf5 After 26...♖dd8, 27.d4 is crushing anyway – so he may as well be hanged for a sheep.

27.exf5 ♖d8 28.♕c4 ♘d5 29.♕e4 ♕g5 30.f4 ♕h6 31.h3

It's game over by this stage, but Nepo struggled on until his resignation on move 44.

Fan-favourite

After losing to Mamedyarov in the Riga final, Maxime Vachier-Lagrave was the fan-favourite to once again do well in Hamburg, and the Frenchman didn't disappoint by scoring a rela-tively comfortable 1½-½ first round victory over China's Wei Yi, the high-light being a subtle bit of endgame play in the opening game.

Maxime Vachier-Lagrave
Wei Yi
Hamburg 2019 (1.1)

position after 32...♖c7

The more material that's traded, the more problematic the a-pawn will become. MVL skilfully finds a way to reach a winnable endgame.

33.♗c4! ♖xb5 34.♗xb5 ♖xc3 35.♗f1

Ideally, Black would like to put his rook behind the a-pawn, but White avoids this with the back-rank threats defended, the a-pawn defended, and the e5-pawn under attack.

35...♖c5 36.♖a1 It is just going to be a matter of technique now.

36...♗a8 37.♗e2

Covering f3 and making way for the king shuffle to safety with ♔f1-e1-d2.

37...e4 38.♔f1 ♔f6 39.♔e1 ♔e5 40.♔d2 f5 41.♖b1

41...g5? The best practical saving chance Wei Yi has is to push his kingside pawns up the board, looking to exchange them all off, and then, if the worst comes to the worst, sacrifice the bishop for the a-pawn to try to get to a ♖+♗ v ♖ ending. But he's too hasty and first had to play 41...♗d5 42.♖b5 ♖c7 43.♗d1 ♖d4 44.♖b4+ ♔c5 45.♖b8 and try to make his stand here.

42.♖b5! The bishop ending is the more practical chance to win; the key being the decoy of the a-pawn.

42...♖d4 43.♖xc5 ♔xc5 44.♔e3 ♗c6 45.♗h5!

45...♔d5 The point to MVL's play is that if Wei goes for the a-pawn with 45...♔b6, after 46.♗g6 ♗d7 47.♔d4 the king comes to e5, with an easily won ending.

46.a7 Now Wei's bishop must stay on the diagonal to cover the a8-queening square.

46...♔e5 47.f4+

Wei resigned in view of 47...♔e6 48.g4! ♔f6 (if 48...gxf4+ 49.♔xf4 fxg4 50.♗g6! e3 51.♔xe3 ♔e5 52.♗h5 ♔f5 53.♔d4 followed by ♗f7-d5 wins) 49.♗e8! ♗d5 50.♗d7 fxg4 51.♗xg4 ♗c6 52.fxg5+ hxg5 53.♔d4 ♗a8 54.♗d1 ♔f5 55.♗b3, and the inevitable ♗d5 next.

That win put MVL and Grischuk on a collision course for a big semi-final showdown, and indeed both got there. Their mini-match proved to be quite a tussle and was decided by what turned out to be an endgame masterclass from Grischuk.

NOTES BY
Anish Giri

Alexander Grischuk
Maxime Vachier-Lagrave
Hamburg 2019 (3.2)
English Opening, Symmetrical Variation

1.♘f3 ♘f6 2.c4 c5 3.♘c3 d5 4.cxd5 ♘xd5 5.e3 e6

The key game of the Hamburg GP was the second classical game between Alexander Grischuk and Maxime Vachier-Lagrave. Because MVL's bishop didn't go to g7?

This is the first time that Maxime Vachier-Lagrave did not try to put the bishop on g7 in this line. Maybe for the better, but not this time. Alexander Grischuk remembered a similar situation, in which he played a 6.♗g5 Najdorf against MVL in the Isle of Man. There, too, Maxime switched lines and deviated from his normal repertoire, but there, too, his first attempt was unsuccessful.
6.♗c4 ♗e7 7.0-0 0-0 8.♕e2
Cunningly delaying the natural d2-d4. This was first played by

Michael Adams, and taken up by a few other players.
8...♘c6 9.♖d1 b6 10.d4 ♘xc3
A natural enough response, but I am not sure this is the way to go in this line. **11.bxc3 ♕c7 12.e4 ♖d8 13.♗e3 ♘a5**

Typically, despite the bishop not being on g7, the lifetime Grünfeld player MVL still manages to make it look like one. Of course, ...♕c7, ...♖d8 and ...♘a5 are the main ideas in the ♗c4 Grünfeld, but here they don't seem to guarantee enough counterplay.

14.♗d3 ♗b7 15.h4

15...b5!?
A typically resourceful MVL shot.
16.♗xb5
Clarifying the position, and why not?
16...♗xe4 17.dxc5

17...♗xf3
Instead, 17...♗xc5 18.♗xc5 ♕xc5 19.♕xe4 ♕xb5 is slightly worse,

Their mini-match proved to be quite a tussle and was decided by what turned out to be an endgame masterclass from Grischuk.

since it leaves Black uncoordinated, particularly in view of the misplaced knight on a5.

18.♕xf3 ♗xc5 19.♗f4 ♕b7
20.♕e2 The endgame after 20.♕xb7 is better for White, but so is this.
20...♕e7 21.h5

21...♗d6 21...h6 looks more natural, but then ♗d3-♕e4-♕h7+ would be hard to counter. **22.♗xd6 ♖xd6 23.♖xd6 ♕xd6 24.♖d1 ♕c5**

25.♖d7 White gives up the c3-pawn for domination. Beautiful.
25...♕xc3 26.♕d1
26.♕e4! is more machine-approved.
26...h6 27.g3 ♖f8
27...♖b8!? was a better defence. After 28.a4 ♘c6 29.♖c7, 29...♕d4! is a little cheapo needed to restore the harmony.
28.♖xa7

Now it's the classical bishop vs knight issue. The passed a-pawn is a tough challenge for the knight.
28...♘c6 29.♖d7 ♘e5 30.♖d8 ♕c7 31.♖xf8+ ♔xf8 32.a4 ♔e7 33.♗e2 ♕c3 34.♕b1 ♘c6 35.♕b7+ ♔f6 36.♗f1 ♘a5 37.♕d7 g5
The kingside structure has been bugging Black for much of the game and this solution is not a happy one.

It only undermines Black's kingside pawn structure even further.

38.hxg6 ♔xg6 39.♔g2 ♔g7 40.♗b5 ♕e5 41.♕d3 ♕c5 42.♕f3 ♕d4 43.♗e8

43...♕d5
This is not an endgame column, but given Black's issues in this one – the outside passer and a bunch of weak

pawns – I expect there were no realistic chances for him to survive.

44.♕xd5 exd5 45.♔f3 ♔f6 46.♔g4 ♔e7 47.♗b5 ♔f6 48.♔h5 ♔g7 49.♗f1 ♘b3 50.♗g2 d4 51.♗f1 ♘d2 52.♗d3 ♘b3 53.♗f1 ♘d2 54.♗d3 ♘b3 55.♗b5

55...f6

A temporary solution. After 55...♘a5 56.♔g4! the king walks over to gobble up the d-pawn, which is the point of the peculiar bishop moves.

56.♗f1 ♘a5 57.♗a6 ♘b3 58.♗b5

Back to the zugzwang.

58...♘a5 59.♔g4

The king is returning at the best time – when the knight is furthest away from the centre.

59...♘b7 60.♔f4 ♘c5 61.a5 d3 62.♔e3 d2

63.♗e2!

The last finesse. The only thing the knight is good for in this kind of endgame is a cheap fork (after 63.♔xd2), and with this bishop retreat, White stops precisely this from happening.
Black resigned.

Breakthrough year

The other semi-final was an intriguing head-to-head between Duda and Daniil Dubov that ended in great disappointment for the latter.

**Daniil Dubov
Jan-Krzysztof Duda**
Hamburg 2019 (3.4)

position after 45...♖f7

The fascinating semi-final struggle between the two more youthful combatants had ended in two draws in 'regular time'. Now Duda, after losing the first tiebreak game, was in a 'must-win' scenario, and at one stage looked close to doing so in the complex middlegame. But a relieved Dubov was glad to be able to play his next move, as the forced trade of queens and a set of minor pieces considerably eases the pressure on his position.

46.♕e5! ♘xf3+ 47.♖xf3 ♕xe5 48.♘xe5 ♖f6 49.♘xc6 ♖xc6 50.♖xf5

The rook and pawn ending should just be a draw – and this is all Dubov needs to go forward to the final. But he has to tread a little carefully, as Duda's pawn chain d5-b3 is the more menacing and could well be winning in a tricky ♖+♙ (or even ♔+♙) ending.

50...a4 51.♖f7+ ♔g8 52.♖a7 ♖e6 53.♔f2 ♖f6+ 54.♔e2 ♖f5 55.♖xa4

The semi-final between Jan-Krzysztof Duda and Daniil Dubov was an intriguing clash that ended in great disappointment for the latter.

♖xh5 56.♖a1 ♖g5 57.♔f3 ♖f5+
58.♔e2 ♔g7 59.♔e3 h5 60.♔e2
♔g6 61.♖a8 ♖f7 62.♖a5 ♖d7
63.♔f3 ♔g5 64.g3 ♖d8 65.♖b5
♖f8+ 66.♔g2

66...♔f5!?

With the players down to their last few
minutes (plus increment), and Duda
needing to win, he goes all-in on a big
bluff in the ♖+♙ ending – and it pays
off! In normal circumstances, we
would have expected to see 66...♖f5
67.♖b8 ♖f7 68.♖d8 ♖f5 69.♖g8+
♔f6 70.♖h8 ♔g5 71.♖g8+ ♔f6 and
a draw.

67.♖xd5+ ♔e4

68.♖e5+??

What a dramatic table-turner! Dubov
suddenly panics when faced with the
bluff of ...♔e3 and ...♖f2+ and hitting
the base of the pawn chain on b2. He
fails to realize that he could simply
first capture the h-pawn. After
68.♖xh5! ♔e3 69.♖e5+ ♔d2 70.g4!
♔c2 71.♖e2+ ♔d3 the simple 72.♖f2!
will draw and would have seen him
through to the final, as the trade of
rooks followed by ...♔c2xb2 allows
the g- and d-pawns to run.

68...♔d3

69.d5?

The only try was 69.♖e1 ♔c2
70.♖e2+ ♔d1 71.♖e5 ♖a8 72.♔f3,
but even here, after 72...♔c1 73.♖e2
♖a2 74.d5 ♖xb2 75.♖xb2 ♔xb2 76.d6
♔c2 77.d7 b2 78.d8♕ b1♕ Black has
a clear winning advantage due to the
weak c3-pawn.

**69...♔c2 70.♖e2+ ♔d1 71.♖e5
♔c1!**

72.♖e4

The (full) point is that now 72.♖e2 is
met by 72...♖d8 and the d-pawn falls,
and with it, the game.

**72...♖d8 73.♖xc4 ♖xd5 74.♖d4
♖c5 75.c4 ♔xb2 76.♖d5**

It's desperation time now.

**76...♖xc4 77.♖xh5 ♔c3 78.♖h1
b2 79.♔h3 ♔b3 80.♖b1 ♖c1
81.♖xb2+ ♔xb2**

The g-pawn is not far enough up the
board for the rook sacrifice to draw.

**82.♔g4 ♔c3 83.♔f5 ♖f1+
84.♔e5 ♖g1 85.♔f4 ♔d4**

White resigned.

After that sore loss, the spirit of a
clearly crestfallen Dubov had well
and truly been broken, and any
dreams he may have harboured of
adding to his breakthrough year by
appearing in an all-Russian final
quickly evaporated. Duda first easily
held the draw and then won the next
tiebreak game for a 3½-2½ victory.

Like Dubov, Duda is clearly having
a big breakthrough year with his
exciting brand of chess. The final
between Duda and Grischuk started
with two quasi-interesting draws.
Duda struck first blood in the rapid
tiebreak decider, only for Grischuk to
hit back with a brace of powerhouse
wins to go on to seal a 3½-2½ victory.
The crucial win is rightly being
described by Anish Giri as having
something of a fairy-tale end to it.

	FIDE GP 2019 – standings	1	2	3	total	prize money
1	Alexander Grischuk	7	3	10	20	€48,000
2	Maxime Vachier-Lagrave		8	5	13	€24,000
3	Shakhriyar Mamedyarov	0	10		10	€29,000
4	Ian Nepomniachtchi	9		0	9	€29,000
5	Jan-Krzysztof Duda	0	1	7	8	€27,000
6	Daniil Dubov	2	0	3	5	€23,000
7	Radoslaw Wojtaszek	5		0	5	€15,000
8	Peter Svidler	2	0	2	4	€21,000
9	Wesley So	1	3		4	€18,000
10	Hikaru Nakamura	3	0	0	3	€20,000
11	Veselin Topalov		1	2	3	€16,000
12	Yu Yangyi		1	1	2	€16,000
13	Wei Yi	2		0	2	€13,000
14	Sergey Karjakin	0	1		1	€13,000
	David Navara		0	1	1	€13,000
16	Nikita Vitiugov	0	0	0	0	€15,000
17	Teimour Radjabov	0		0	0	€10,000
	Anish Giri	0	0		0	€10,000
	Dmitry Jakovenko	0		0	0	€10,000
	Levon Aronian	0	0		0	€10,000
	Pentala Harikrishna	0	0	0	0	€10,000

1=Moscow; 2=Riga; 3=Hamburg (To play: Jerusalem)

NOTES BY
Anish Giri

Alexander Grischuk
Jan-Krzysztof Duda
Hamburg 2019 (4.4)
Queen's Indian, Nimzowitsch Variation

1.d4 ♘f6 2.c4 e6 3.♘f3 b6 4.g3 ♗a6

The Queen's Indian was JKD's main line of defence for this match.
5.b3 ♗b4+ 6.♗d2 ♗e7 7.♗g2 d5 8.0-0 0-0 9.♘e5 c6 10.♗c3 ♘fd7

11.♘d3!? A rare idea, which seemed to take Duda by surprise. Always nice to have something ready for a must-win game. **11...dxc4 12.♘b4 cxb3** 12...♕c8!? could be an improvement, but what do I know? **13.♘xa6 ♘xa6 14.♗xc6**

14...♖b8
Now Black ends up losing a pawn without compensation.
14...♖c8 15.♗b7 ♖xc3 16.♘xc3 b2 17.♖b1 ♕c7 18.♘d5 exd5 19.♗xa6 ♕c3 leaves a mess, but I am not sure this is the solution for Black.
15.axb3 ♘b4 16.♗xb4 ♗xb4 17.♖xa7
The rest is, quite frankly, a matter of technique, converting the extra pawn to a win, and Alexander Grischuk's got plenty of technique.

17...♘f6 18.e3 ♖c8 19.♗g2 ♖e8 20.♘d2 ♖e7 21.♖xe7 ♗xe7 22.♘c4
With the knight developed, there is nothing to hold White back from a smooth conversion.
22...♗f8 23.♕a1 b5 24.♘e5 ♕b6 25.♖c1

As long as White doesn't trade the knights, the opposite-coloured bishops make for a completely non-drawish endgame.
25...♖xc1+ 26.♕xc1 ♕a7 27.♕c8 b4 28.♗b7 ♕a1+ 29.♔g2 ♕a5 30.♗c6 ♕a7

31.♗e8 ♘xe8 32.♘d7!
A nice clincher. All fairy-tales end with a pretty blow like this one! Black resigned. ■

Alexander Grischuk will not play in the final GP in Jerusalem, but the Russian looks to be excellently placed to qualify for the Candidates Tournament.

Wang Hao wins Grand Swiss in great style

Former prodigy is second Chinese to qualify for Candidates

The FIDE Grand Swiss in Isle of Man attracted a formidable field. Small wonder, with a $433,000 prize-fund and a spot in the Candidates tournament at stake. Even Magnus Carlsen and Fabiano Caruana took part, adding a controversial dimension to the fight for that highly coveted ticket (which they didn't need). But they, too, had to bow to an impressive Wang Hao who, at the age of 30, played the tournament of his life. **ERWIN L'AMI** reports.

MARIA EMELIANOVA

I n my chess career it had never happened that I scored 5½ out of 11 in an Open tournament, ended up sharing 65th to 104th place, still gained rating points and was reasonably satisfied with the outcome. But this is exactly what happened in the FIDE Grand Swiss tournament in Isle of Man.

Over the past several years, the Isle of Man has hosted one of the best annual Opens in the circuit; one that even the world elite is happy to join. This year saw the event as we have come to know it transformed into the 'FIDE Grand Swiss'. The idea was straightforward: the 100 best players in the world received an invite based on their average rating this year, and 50 more players were added by the organizer and by FIDE. The winner of the 11-round event was guaranteed a much-coveted spot in the Candidates tournament next March!

As a result, the FIDE Grand Swiss will go into the books as the strongest open tournament ever, with virtually the entire world elite participating.

The venue at the Comis Hotel and Golf Resort consisted of two playing halls. In the first hall, Boards 1 to 34 were situated, while the second hall accommodated the remaining games. This meant that for most players it was not so much the fight for the Candidates that mattered as the fight to get into the first hall! As for myself, I lost that fight after Round 3, never to return to the first hall again! So imagine my surprise in Round 8, when the door of our hall suddenly opened, and Alexei Shirov and Yu Yangyi entered, closely followed by the arbiter. Knowing that both players were sitting at the top table that day, I was intrigued by what happened next. Both sat down at one of the reserve boards and continued playing from what looked like an extremely sharp Sicilian position. Little did I know that a game between Karjakin and Dreev next to Shirov and Yu Yangyi had caused this move

to another hall. It was only after I had finished my own game that I heard that both games had taken an identical course and that the arbiter had decided to relocate one of them! I have often wondered what would happen in team events if Boards 1 and 2, and Boards 3 and 4 would copy each other – effectively making it possible to draw any match you like – but in Isle of Man they apparently know how to handle such situations!

Undefeated streak

The big favourite in Isle of Man was Magnus Carlsen, as in any event that he participates in. Magnus is expected to win anything he plays these days, but in this event he had to settle for a 'modest' 2825 performance. He did go through the event undefeated, meaning that Sergei Tiviakov's world record of 110 games without a loss is under serious pressure! At the moment Magnus

Carlsen is at 102 games without a loss. I liked the following game from Round 6.

Magnus Carlsen
Alexei Shirov
Douglas 2019 (6)
Petroff, Steinitz Variation

1.e4 e5 2.♘f3 ♘f6 3.d4 ♘xe4 4.♗d3 d5 5.♘xe5 ♘d7 6.♘c3 ♘xe5 7.dxe5

A trendy way of playing for White in this variation of the Petroff. Shirov

For most players it was not so much the fight for the Candidates that mattered as the fight to get into the first hall!

Magnus Carlsen remained undefeated at the Grand Swiss, but shared third place was not what he had come to Isle of Man for.

now follows the 'classical' route where Wang Hao went 7...♗b4 against Anand later in the tournament.

7...♘xc3 8.bxc3 This position used to be considered harmless for Black, but it's probably not. I would recommend having a look at Nikita Vitiugov's excellent analysis of his win versus Wesley So in the previous magazine (New In Chess 2019/7), which involved the same line.

8...♗e7 9.0-0 0-0 10.f4 f5 11.♗e3

11...c5 New compared to 11...♗e6, which was seen in Vitiugov-So, Khanty-Mansiysk 2019. The game continuation doesn't change the nature of the position much.

12.♗e2

White's play is very straightforward. First the bishop is rerouted to f3 in order to pressurize the d-pawn.

12...♗e6 13.♗f3 ♕d7 14.a4

It would be very nice for Black to get ...b7-b5 in, so Carlsen prevents it.

14...♖ad8 15.♕e2 ♕c7 16.♖fb1!? b6 17.♖d1

This was probably White's plan: provoke ...b6 to prevent the queen from reaching a5, and then move the b-rook to d1. Also interesting

was 17.a5!?, softening up Black's queenside.

17...g5 I like this attempt at counterplay. If Black does nothing, White will continue piling up on the d-pawn. **18.h3 ♖d7 19.♖d2** 19.a5!? once again looked good, but Carlsen seems to have made the call not to push his a-pawn. **19...♖fd8 20.♖ad1**

20...gxf4 Changing the move order with 20...d4! 21.cxd4 gxf4 22.♗xf4 ♖xd4 23.♖xd4 cxd4 would have kept White's advantage to a minimum.

21.♗xf4 d4

22.♕f2! The difference is immediately apparent. White is in no need to take on d4.

22...♔h8 Because of the queen check on g3, taking on c3 is of course out of the question: 22...dxc3? 23.♕g3+ ♔h8 24.♖xd7 ♖xd7 25.♗d6!.

23.♔h1 ♕c8 24.♔h2

24...♖g8 It was better to sit tight with 24...♕c7. The game continuation allows Magnus to make progress. **25.cxd4 cxd4 26.♖xd4 ♖xd4**

27.♖xd4! A very strong exchange sac. **27...♗c5 28.c3** Even stronger is 28.♕h4 ♗xd4 29.♕f6+ ♖g7 30.♗h6! ♕d7 31.♗xg7+ ♕xg7 32.♕d8+ ♕g8 33.♕xd4, with a winning position. The game continuation is good too, though. Carlsen uses tactics to make sure Shirov can't blockade the central pawns. **28...♗xd4 29.cxd4 ♕d7 30.♕d2 ♗d5 31.e6!**

The point, making the bishop on f4 come alive.

31...♛xe6 32.♗e5+ ♖g7 33.♛c3 ♗xf3 34.♛xf3

34...♛e8 More tenacious was 34...h5 35.♛a8+ ♔h7 36.♗xg7 ♔xg7 37.♛xa7+ ♔g6, but – at least practically speaking – the position seems very hard to hold for Black.

35.♛xf5 ♔g8 36.♗xg7 ♔xg7 37.♛g5+ ♔f8 38.♛f4+ ♔e7 39.♛e4+ ♔f8

40.♛xh7

40.♛xe8+ ♔xe8 41.♔g3 a5!, followed by ... b6-b5, and Black draws, would be awkward!

40...♛xa4 41.♛f5+ ♔g7 42.♛e5+ ♔f7 43.h4

Black resigned. White's pawns are more advanced, which makes the queen ending hopeless. A sample line is 43....a5 44.h5 ♛d7 45.d5 a4 46.h6 ♔g6 47.♛e6+!, and after the queen swap White is ahead in the pawn race.

Spanish star

In massive events like these, it is always nice to look for new faces at the top. Of course, the usual suspects were playing on the top boards for the entire event, but I think the tournament also marked the breakthrough of a few players. First of all, Spanish star David Anton should be mentioned. He had already made quite a name for himself in the Gibraltar tournament earlier this year. In Isle of Man, Anton showed that, in his best form, he can compete with the very best. After eight rounds he saw himself in the shared lead after the following amazing game against Alexander Grischuk.

David Anton
Alexander Grischuk
Douglas 2019 (8)
English Opening, Reversed Sicilian

1.c4 e5 2.g3 ♘f6 3.♗g2 ♗c5 4.♘c3 c6

This aggressive approach, aiming for central action, fits an earlier statement of Grischuk's that after 1.c4 e5 Black should be able to play on equal terms.

5.♘f3

5.e3 0-0 6.♘ge2 d5 7.cxd5 ♘xd5 8.d4 exd4 9.♘xd5 cxd5 10.♘xd4 has been seen in a couple of games, but is

totally harmless. Anton's reply is the real test of this system.

5...e4 6.♘h4 d5 7.cxd5 cxd5 8.d3 ♘g4 9.0-0 g5

Both players have been striving for this position. Black is horribly over-extended, but with his last move he has trapped the knight on h4.

10.d4 ♗e7

10...♗b6!? would stop 11.h3, as now 11...gxh4 12.gxh4 ♘c6! is strong, pressuring d4. White has better though, with 11.♘f3!?, the idea being 11...exf3 12.exf3 ♘f6 13.♗xg5 h6 14.♗h4 0-0 15.f4

ANALYSIS DIAGRAM

with huge compensation. 16.♘xd5 is a threat and after, for example, 15...♘c6 (15...♕d6 16.♘b5!) 16.♘xd5 ♗xd4 17.♕xd4! ♘xd4 18.♗xf6 ♕a5 19.♗xd4, with just two pieces for the queen, White is neverthe-less dominating. Perhaps 11...h6!? (after 11.♘f3!?) is the way forward for Black when 12.♘e5 ♘xe5 13.dxe5 ♗e6 14.♔h1 ♘c6 15.f4 ♕d7 offers good chances of resistance. There is nothing wrong with the game contin-uation, though.

11.h3

David Anton won an amazing game against Alexander Grischuk. It was painful for the Spaniard that he spoiled his chances for the Candidates with a loss against, of all persons, Fabiano Caruana.

11...♘xf2 This move was widely condemned but I believe that's too harsh. The alternative 11...gxh4 12.hxg4 leads to extremely messy complications following both 12...♘c6 and 12...hxg3.

12.♖xf2 gxh4 13.♕b3

13...hxg3

This is probably a mistake. With 13...♗e6! 14.♕xb7 ♕d7! 15.♕xa8 0-0

ANALYSIS DIAGRAM

Black could have asked some tough questions. White's queen is confined on a8 and with Black's centre still intact I believe the position is far from clear. The line continues 16.♗h6 ♖d8 17.♘xe4 ♘a6! 18.♕xd8+ ♕xd8 19.♘c3 hxg3 20.♖f3 ♗d6, and with the g3-pawn still alive, I think Black is alright.

14.♖f4

14...♘c6 The big difference after 14...♗e6 15.♕xb7 ♕d7 16.♕xa8 0-0 is 17.♖g4+! ♗xg4 (or 17...♔h8 18.♗h6! ♖d8 19.♗g7+ ♔g8 20.♗e5+ ♗xg4 21.♗xb8) 18.♕xd5, and the queen escapes! That's why including 13...hxg3 14.♖f4 is not to Black's advantage.

15.♕xd5

15...f5 15...♕xd5 16.♘xd5 f5 is an enterprising way to continue the fight for the initiative, but after the logical 17.♘c7+ ♔f7 18.♘xa8 ♘xd4 19.♖f1 Black doesn't quite have enough compensation for the rook.

16.♗xe4! An important follow-up. After any other move Black is simply better.

16...fxe4
This loses swiftly. 16...♘xd4 17.♗d3! is also hugely unpleasant, but 16...♕xd5 17.♗xd5 ♗d7, despite surely being better for White, would still be a game in which there is all to play for.

17.♕h5+ ♔d7 18.♗e3
Calmly finishing his development. Black is hopelessly lost with the king on d7.

Inviting the World Champion and his latest Challenger was a very questionable decision.

18...♕g8 19.d5 ♘d8 20.♘xe4 ♕g6 21.♘e5 ♘f7 22.♖xf7! Power play! **22...♕xf7 23.♖c1 ♖f8 24.♗g5!**

Very pretty. Since 24...♗xg5 runs into 25.♕c7+ ♔e8 26.♘d6 mate, Black resigned.

In Round 9, Anton drew with Levon Aronian with the black pieces, but he found his nemesis the next day in Fabiano Caruana when, doubling Black, he was ground down in an endgame. This loss signalled the end of Anton's Candidates ambitions. Allow me some words of criticism at this point. Even though everybody – including myself – loved seeing World Champion Magnus Carlsen and his most recent Challenger Fabiano Caruana compete in Isle of Man, I think that inviting them was a very questionable decision. The World Champion is already seeded in next year's World Championship match, while Caruana will automat-

ically receive a spot in the Candidates tournament in Yekaterinburg, Russia, next March, after reaching the final of the previous cycle. This makes it very odd for either of them to be allowed to influence who qualifies for the Candidates. The argument that the participation of the numbers 1 and 2 in the world rankings added legitimacy to the event is way too thin. Who knows what would have happened if Anton had faced a different opponent in Round 10?

Alekseenko joins 2700 Club
Someone else worthy of attention is 22-year-old Kirill Alekseenko. The Russian has made a huge jump recently, and after this event has become a member of the 2700 Club. It was remarkable to see the ease with which Alekseenko played on the top boards – as if he had played dozens of such events before! In Round 10 he won a crucial game against Sergey Karjakin, which made him one of the few players with a chance of the Candidates spot in the final round the next day.

Sergey Karjakin
Kirill Alekseenko
Douglas 2019 (10)
Réti Opening, Barcza System
1.♘f3 d5 2.g3 ♘d7 3.d4 ♘b6

A remarkable move that I had not seen before. There is surely some logic behind it, as Black effectively stops White from getting c2-c4 in.

4.♗g2

4.♘bd2!? could be a trickier move order, to meet 4...♗f5 with 5.♘h4 ♗g4 6.h3 ♗h5 7.♘g2!, since the g2-square is still available. Black will probably have to go 5...e6.

4...♗f5 5.0-0 Now 5.♘h4 ♗g4 6.h3 ♗h5 7.g4 e6! will lead nowhere.

5...e6 6.♘e5

6...c6 Something curious happened here, as Alekseenko spent 42 minutes on this move...

7.c4 f6

... and 22 minutes on this one – justifiably, though, because his 7th move sets the board on fire. It essentially forces White to sacrifice a piece. 7...♘f6 was the more restrained option.

8.cxd5 fxe5 9.dxc6

9...e4 9...bxc6 10.♗xc6+ ♔f7 11.♗xa8 ♕xa8 would be great for Black, but White first includes 11.e4! ♗g6, and now 12.♗xa8 ♕xa8 13.f4! is a wholly different ball game.

10.cxb7 ♖b8

All forced from 7...f6 onwards.

11.♘c3 The alternative was 11.f3!? when, after 11...♘f6 (11... exf3 12.♗xf3 keeps the b7-pawn alive) 12.fxe4 ♗xe4 13.♖xf6! ♗xg2

14.♖xe6+ ♗e7 15.♗g5 ♖xb7 16.♗xe7 ♖xe7 17.♖xe7+ ♕xe7 18.♔xg2 ♕e4+ 19.♔g1 ♕e3+ 20.♔g2

ANALYSIS DIAGRAM

it's a draw by perpetual check.

11...♘f6 12.♗g5 ♗e7 13.♗xf6 ♗xf6 14.♘xe4 ♗xe4 15.♗xe4 ♕xd4 16.♕c2

White has three pawns for the piece and especially the b7-pawn looks

MARIA EMELIANOVA

Twenty-two-year-old Kirill Alekseenko has made a great jump recently and after the Grand Swiss he joined the 2700 Club.

continuation prevents the a1-rook to get to c1.

21.♖d1 ♘c5 22.♖7d2

Or 22.♖c7 ♗e5 23.♖c8+ ♔e7, when Black has everything under control.

22...♔f7 23.♖c2 ♗e7

Having picked up a pawn, Black is now firmly in the driver's seat. But the game is far from over, especially when you play the Minister of Defence.

24.♖b1 ♖hd8 25.♖b5

It was probably better for White to await further developments and simply improve his position with small moves like h4, ♔g2, e3 etc.

25...♘a6! The knight will actually move to greener pastures.

26.♗f3 ♘b4 27.♖c4 ♘d5 28.♖c6 ♖d7 29.♗g4 ♘c7 30.♖b3

juicy. The presence of opposite-coloured bishops makes the position even more intriguing.

Optically I'd rather be White here, but Alekseenko makes a very good case for Black's position in the remainder of the game.

16...♕c4 16...0-0!? was also worth considering, since 17.♗xh7+ ♔h8 18.♗e4 ♘d5! picks up the b7-pawn.

17.♕xc4 From here on in, things start going downhill for White. Better was 17.♗c6+ ♔e7 18.♖ac1! ♕xc2 19.♖xc2, when White will slowly bring his queenside pawns forward and should have a risk-free endgame.

17...♘xc4 18.♖fd1 ♘xb2 19.♗c6+ ♔f8 20.♖d7

20...♘d3! White must have missed this move. Instead, 20...♘c4 21.♖c1 ♘e5 (21...♘b6 22.♖d3 ♔e7 23.♖cd1! makes it hard for Black to move) 22.♖c7 ♘xc6 23.♖1xc6 ♗e5 24.♖d7

ANALYSIS DIAGRAM

with the dominating white rooks spelling trouble for Black. The game

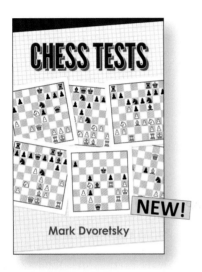
30...♗d6
Time-trouble starts to interfere with the play at this point. The computer indicates the excellent regrouping ...♗d8, ...♔e7 and ...♖d6!

31.♗f3
31.e4!, with the idea of expanding with f2-f4 and e4-e5, was the way to punish Black for his 30th move.

31...♘d5 32.♔g2 ♔e7 33.♗xd5 exd5 34.♖e3+ ♔f7 35.♖f3+ ♔e7 36.♖e3+ ♔f6 37.♖f3+ ♔e6 38.♖e3+ ♔f6 39.♖f3+ ♔e5 40.♖e3+ ♔f5

With move 40 reached, Alekseenko can calmly figure out the winning plan.

41.♖f3+ ♔e6 42.♖e3+ ♔f7 43.♖f3+ ♔g8 44.♖c8+ ♖d8 45.♖fc3 ♔f7 46.♖3c6 ♔e7 47.♖a6 ♖dxc8 48.bxc8♕ ♖xc8 49.♖xa7+ ♖c7

50.♖a5
Trading rooks is unlikely to hold: 50.♖xc7+ ♗xc7 and now both 51.f4 ♔f6 52.♔f3 g5! 53.e3 ♔f5 54.h3 h6 55.g4+ ♔e6 56.f5+ ♔d6 57.♔e2 ♔c5 58.♔d3 ♗e5 59.♔d2 ♔b4 60.♔c2 ♔a3 61.♔b1 ♗f6 and 51.♔f3 ♗b6

52.e3 g5!? 53.♔e2 g4 54.f3 gxf3+ 55.♔xf3 ♔e6 56.g4 ♔e5 57.h4 ♗d8 58.g5 ♔f5 are winning for Black.

50...♗c5 51.e3

Some words about this endgame. White is quite certainly lost, but if he can reach the endgame of rook and f2, g3 and h4 versus rook, bishop and g7/6, h5 the position is a theoretical draw. That means Karjakin will do his utmost from this point onwards to lure Black's h-pawn forward. That would be a huge step in the direction of a draw.

51...♔d6 52.♖a6+ ♔d7 53.♖a4 ♖a7 54.♖h4 ♖xa2 55.♔f3

55...h6 55...♔e6!? 56.♖xh7 ♗b4! and ...♗e1 would have been clearer.

56.♖g4 ♗f8
Making things more complicated. I like 56...g5 57.h4 ♗e7 58.hxg5 hxg5 59.♖d4 ♔e6, when the winning plan consists of pushing ...g5-g4, carrying out the ...d5-d4 break and sacrificing on f2 in order to get a winning pawn ending. Note that with pawns on g6 and h5, Black can never carry out this plan of obtaining a winning pawn endgame, which is why provoking the pawn to h5 is so essential.

57.♖f4 ♗e7 58.♖f7 g6

59.h4

59.♖h7!? h5 would have forced the desired push. Now White needs to play h2-h4 and make sure his rook will not get trapped:

– 60.♖g7 ♖a6 61.h4 ♖f6+ 62.♔g2, and although White's rook is almost trapped, it is still alive. It's not clear to me if, and how, Black will win.

– 60.♖h8? is too hasty and allows Black to win: 60...♗b4 61.♔g2 ♗e1 62.♖f8 ♔e7 63.♖f4 ♗c3! (White's rook is running out of squares) 64.h4 ♖b2! 65.♖a4 ♗e1 66.♖f4 ♖b4 67.♖f3

ANALYSIS DIAGRAM

and now it's very simple, 67...♗c3

68.♔g1 ♗e5 69.♔g2 ♖b6 and ...♖f6, with a win.

– 60.h4 ♔e6! runs into similar issues. There is no stopping ...♗b4-e1.

59...♖a6 59...♔e6! 60.♖h7 h5, followed by ...♗b4, would once again win on the spot.

60.♖h7 ♖f6+ 61.♔g2 h5

62.♖h8 Now the rook does get trapped! 62.♖g7! would transpose to my note on move 59.

62...♖f8! Shutting the door on the rook.

63.♖h6 ♖g8 64.♖h7 ♔e6 65.♔g1 ♖f8 66.♖g7 ♔f6 67.♖h7 ♖f7 68.♖h8 ♗f8 69.♖g8 ♔f5 70.♔g2 ♖f6 71.♖h8 ♔e6 72.♖h7 ♖f7 73.♖h8 ♔e7

74.f4 If White keeps waiting with 74.♔g1, 74...♗e8 75.♔g2 ♖e7 followed by ...♔f7! will round up the rook. However, with the pawn on f4 all hopes of a fortress are lost.

74...♖f6 75.♔g8 ♗c5 76.♖d8 ♔e6 77.♖g8 ♔f5 78.♔f3 ♖f8 79.♖g7 ♖e8 80.♖f7+ ♔e6 81.♖b7

81...♖a8 81...♔d6 82.♖b3 ♖xe3+ 83.♖xe3 ♗xe3 84.♔xe3 ♔c5 would have saved some time. **82.♖g7 ♖a3 83.♖xg6+ ♔e7 84.♖g5 ♖xe3+ 85.♔g2 ♔d6 86.♖xh5 d4 87.♖h8 d3**

The d-pawn is unstoppable.
88.h5 ♔d7 89.♖h7+ ♔c6
White resigned.

Blistering pace

Alekseenko was close to winning in the last round as well, but his opponent, Nikita Vitiugov, narrowly escaped in what looked like a very scary knight ending. In that last round, all eyes were on Wang Hao. The 30-year-old Chinese has been around for a long time already and has beaten the best players on the planet. In recent years, though, his rating had dropped a bit, and his compatriots Yu Yangyi and especially Ding Liren have claimed a more prominent role on the world stage.

So far, 2019 had already been a good year for Wang Hao, but his achievement in Isle of Man will certainly make it a year he is unlikely to forget. He set off at a blistering pace, winning his first three games, but it didn't end there. After five rounds he shared the lead with 4 out of 5 before facing off to Luke McShane. The winner takes us through that gem, in which we see Wang Hao at his best, slowly grinding down his opponent.

NOTES BY
Wang Hao

Wang Hao
Luke McShane
Douglas 2019 (6)
Catalan Opening, Bogo-Indian Variation

This game was played in Round 6, when my opponent and I were both in the leading pack. It was clear that Luke McShane was in good form, but since he always has dubious opening preparation, I decided to be solid in hopes of getting a position in which I could exert long-term pressure.

1.d4 ♘f6 2.c4 e6

I had noticed that my opponent had recently started playing 2...e6 instead of his favourite King's Indian, in which I have analysed a lot of ideas for White.

3.g3 ♗b4+ 4.♗d2 c5

> 'Luke McShane was in good form, but since he always has dubious opening preparation, I decided to be solid to get a position in which I could exert long-term pressure.'

In Round 1, Luke had played this 4...c5 move in a Bogo-Indian, when his opponent Yilmaz chose 3.♘f3. That game continued with a similar structure, but the knight on f3 became clumsy when White had to defend the e4-pawn.

5.♗xb4 cxb4 6.♗g2 0-0 7.e4 d6 8.♘e2 ♘c6 Here 8...e5 is more popular, maintaining the possibility for Black to play ...♘a6 later.

9.0-0 ♗d7 10.♕d3 a5 11.♘d2 e5 12.♖fd1 White will slowly improve his position with ♖ac1, ♘f1 and ♘e3. I think that Black needs some active ideas to keep the tension, decisions that are not easy to make over the board.

12...♕b8 Trying to stop ♘f1 (see the note to White's next move). But I was actually happy to see this move, since Black could have tried ...h5 to scupper White's plan.

After 12...♖e8 13.♘f1 h5!? 14.h4

(after 14.h3 h4 15.g4 exd4 16.♘xd4 ♘e5, Black has the idea of ...♘g6 and ...♘f4. And after 14.♘e3 h4, Black will have better chances of counterplay by weakening White's kingside) 14...♖c8 15.♖ac1 exd4 16.♘xd4 ♘e5 the position is dynamically balanced. It's difficult to drive away the e5-knight with f4, since White has a weak kingside.

The immediate 12...h5!? was also good.

13.♖ac1

To prevent ...b5. With the support of the c1-rook, the advance c5 becomes a good possibility against ...b5.

13.♘f1?! would be met by the clever 13...b5!, when after 14.cxb5 ♘d8, Black is totally fine.

It could be a good idea to play 13.a4, stopping ...b5, but I didn't like my isolated pawn on c4 after 13...bxa3 14.bxa3 ♕a7 15.♘f1 (15.d5 ♘b8) 15...exd4 16.♘xd4 ♘e5, although White is actually slightly better here.

13...♕a7

If Black tries to weaken White's kingside with 13...♗g4 14.f3 ♗d7, White can try to play 15.h3, followed by f4.

13...b5 is not a good idea here, because Black has problems in view of the d2-knight jumping to c4: 14.cxb5 ♘a7 15.b6! ♕xb6 (after 15...♘c8 16.dxe5 dxe5 17.♘d4! ♘xb6 18.♘c6,

Black has an unpleasant position) 16.♘c4.

13...♖e8 seems more logical to me. I would have continued with 14.h3 in order to see Black's next move (14.♘f1 doesn't offer much for White after 14...b5 15.c5 dxc5 16.♖xc5 ♕a7 17.♖dc1 ♖ac8 18.d5 ♘e7 19.♖xc8 ♘xc8, when Black has a solid position).

14.♘f1 ♖ac8 15.h3 ♖fd8 16.♘e3

A flashy start and a dashing finish brought Wang Hao first place and qualification to the Candidates Tournament.

I have reached my goal in that I can now press for a long time in a slightly better position. But Black has a solid position and it will be difficult for me to break through.

16...h6 17.b3

17...♕b8?!

I guess that my opponent started losing patience here.

Continuing to wait with 17...♖e8 was probably a better idea. I would try to improve my position slowly with 18.♔h2 ♖cd8 19.♖d2, followed by ♖cd1.

Instead, 18.dxe5 dxe5 19.♘d5 ♘h7 wouldn't hurt Black much.

And 18.f4 is probably too early. After 18...♖cd8! Black will open the centre with some exchanges and put his bishop on c6. If White continues with ambitious ideas like 19.fxe5 dxe5 20.d5, the position after 20...♘b8 21.g4 ♘a6 22.♘g3 ♘c5 23.♕d2 ♖f8 will be unclear.

18.f4!

18.d5 ♘e7 19.a4 was also playable. White can try to create ideas based on his space advantage. But I wanted to maintain the tension in the centre.

18...b5!? My opponent decided to initiate counterplay here.

19.cxb5

19...♘e7 If 19...♘xd4, after 20.♘xd4 ♖xc1 21.♖xc1 exd4 22.♕xd4 ♗xb5 23.♔h2, White has a solid positional advantage thanks to his control of the d5-square and the vulnerability of the d6-pawn.

20.♖xc8 ♖xc8

I had thought that the complications after 18...b5 wouldn't work well for Black, but here I lost my way.

21.dxe5?

The right move was 21.b6!, but after 21...exf4 I had missed 22.e5!, which would be very strong (I had only considered 22.♘xf4, which is also good, but again, I blundered an important move: 22...♘c3 23.♕d2 ♕xb6 24.♘c4 ♕c7 25.e5 ♘e8, and here I missed 26.♘e2!, which would have yielded White a large advantage). After 22...dxe5 23.dxe5 ♕xe5

ANALYSIS DIAGRAM

24.♘c4 (24.♘xf4 ♗c6 25.♘c4 is also excellent for White) 24...♕c5+ 25.♕d4 ♕xd4+ 26.♖xd4 my b-pawn will decide the game.

21...dxe5

22.♕d6?!

22.b6 was probably a better choice, when after 22...♕xb6 23.fxe5 ♘h7 24.♔h2 ♗e6 White is slightly better because of the extra double pawn; but Black has sufficient resources to defend.

22...♗xb5 23.♕xb8 ♖xb8

Now I have lost all my advantage. Fortunately, I could still try an idea to confuse my opponent.

24.fxe5 ♘d7?

And he goes wrong.

Somehow my opponent didn't like his position after 24...♗xe2,

ANALYSIS DIAGRAM

when 25.exf6 looks tempting, but it won't work in view of 25...♗xd1 26.fxe7 ♗e2 27.♔f2! (27.♘f5? ♖e8! – not allowing ♘d6 – 28.e5 ♗b5 29.♘d6 ♖xe7 30.♘xb5 ♖xe5, and only White is playing for a draw here) 27...♗d3 28.♘f5 ♖e8 29.♔e3 ♗a6 30.e5 ♗b5

ANALYSIS DIAGRAM

and now White has a nice move to force a draw with: 31.♔d4! ♗d7 32.♔c5 ♗xf5 33.♔d6 g5 34.♗c6 ♖xe7 35.♔xe7 ♔g7 36.♗d5 ♗b1 37.♔d6 ♗xa2 38.♔c5 a4 39.♔xb4 axb3 40.♗xb3 ♗xb3 41.♔xb3.

And after 25.♖d2 ♘h5 26.♖xe2 ♘xg3 27.♖c2 Black is actually doing fine: 27...♘g6 28.♔f2 ♘h5 29.♖c5 ♘hf4 30.♖xa5 ♘d3+ (after 30...♘xe5?! 31.♗f1 White has some slight chances, because the knight on f4 is somewhat uncoordinated) 31.♔g3 ♘dxe5.

25.e6

After the game Luke told me that he had simply forgotten about this reply. Now Black has a passive position.

25...fxe6 26.♘d4

26...♘e5? The right way was 26...♘f8 to defend the e6-pawn, although White can try to continue to press: 27.♗f1! ♗xf1 (27...♗d7 28.♖c1; 27...♗e8 28.♗c4) 28.♔xf1 a4 29.♔e2 ♖a8 30.♘c4, and Black will have to defend a tough endgame.
27.♘xe6 ♖c8?! 27...♔f7 was better.

28.♘d5? 28.♘f5! was a stronger idea, intending to force Black to swap the knights and open the diagonal for my bishop, after which the game would have finished much faster.
28...♘7g6 I had forgotten that Black can avoid the exchange with this simple move. **29.♘d4 ♗e8**

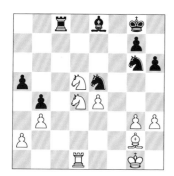

30.♗f1

Luke McShane had a great start, but after he failed to convert a winning position against Fabiano Caruana in Round 5 (and take the lead) he ran out of steam.

30.♔f2 was better, when White has 31.♔e2 to meet 30...♖c1.
30...♗f7 31.♔f2 ♖c5 32.♗g2 Kind of clumsy. 32.♘e3 or 32.♘f4 would have been better.
32...♘f8 33.♔e3 ♘fd7 34.♘e2 I wanted to swap the rooks with ♖c1. 34.♘f3 was probably a slightly better idea, intending to exchange a set of knights and clear the way for my king.

34...♔f8? The last mistake, made under time-pressure, and allowing White to swap the rooks to reach a winning endgame.
34...♖c2 was called for. After 35.♖d2 ♖c5 I am not sure how to break Black's defence. For example: 36.♘d4 ♖c1.
35.♖c1 ♗xd5 36.♖xc5 ♘xc5 37.exd5 ♔e7 38.♘d4 ♘b7 39.♔e4 ♘d7 40.♔d3 ♘e5+ 41.♔e4

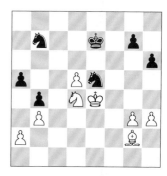

After getting 50 minutes more on the clock I realized that I was going to win this tough game. White is totally winning here because of his extra pawn and Black's weak pawn structure.
41...♘d7 42.♘c6+ ♔d6 43.♔d4 ♔c7 44.♗f3

Since the two knights are clumsy, Black had to weaken his own position.

Douglas 2019

				TPR
1	Wang Hao	CHN 2726	8	2900
2	Fabiano Caruana	USA 2812	8	2888
3	Kirill Alekseenko	RUS 2674	7½	2834
4	Levon Aronian	ARM 2758	7½	2833
5	David Anton	ESP 2674	7½	2821
6	Magnus Carlsen	NOR 2876	7½	2825
7	Hikaru Nakamura	USA 2745	7½	2803
8	Nikita Vitiugov	RUS 2732	7½	2792
9	Alexander Grischuk	RUS 2759	7	2779
10	David Paravyan	RUS 2602	7	2774
11	David Howell	ENG 2694	7	2743
12	Vidit Gujrathi	IND 2718	7	2743
13	Le Quang Liem	VIE 2708	7	2722
14	Parham Maghsoodloo	IRI 2664	6½	2748
15	Nijat Abasov	AZE 2632	6½	2745
16	Vladislav Kovalev	BLR 2661	6½	2741
17	Vladimir Fedoseev	RUS 2664	6½	2738
18	Aleksandr Rakhmanov	RUS 2621	6½	2730
19	Yuriy Kryvoruchko	UKR 2669	6½	2729
20	Constantin Lupulescu	ROU 2643	6½	2702
21	Hrant Melkumyan	ARM 2650	6½	2719
22	Maxim Matlakov	RUS 2716	6½	2728
23	Sergey Karjakin	RUS 2760	6½	2707
24	Yu Yangyi	CHN 2763	6½	2720
25	Yuriy Kuzubov	UKR 2636	6½	2696
26	Vishy Anand	IND 2765	6½	2707
27	Wesley So	USA 2767	6½	2705
28	Radoslaw Wojtaszek	POL 2748	6½	2714
29	Peter Svidler	RUS 2729	6½	2710
30	Nguyen Ngoc Truong Son	VIE 2638	6½	2663
31	Samuel Sevian	USA 2654	6½	2688
32	Jeffery Xiong	USA 2708	6½	2703
33	Pentala Harikrishna	IND 2748	6½	2698
34	Ray Robson	USA 2670	6½	2686
35	Grigoriy Oparin	RUS 2654	6½	2683
36	Sethuraman S.P.	IND 2624	6½	2677
37	Robert Hovhannisyan	ARM 2639	6½	2667
38	Paco Vallejo	ESP 2694	6½	2691
39	Nils Grandelius	SWE 2691	6½	2673
40	Aleksey Dreev	RUS 2662	6½	2663
41	Krishnan Sasikiran	IND 2675	6½	2659
42	Peter Leko	HUN 2670	6½	2655
43	Alexey Sarana	RUS 2655	6	2720
44	Evgeniy Najer	RUS 2635	6	2694
45	Bogdan-Daniel Deac	ROU 2613	6	2720
46	Nodirbek Abdusattorov	UZB 2608	6	2712
47	Narayanan.S.L	IND 2611	6	2704
48	Dommaraju Gukesh	IND 2520	6	2683
49	Rinat Jumabayev	KAZ 2630	6	2680
50	Vladimir Akopian	ARM 2638	6	2656
154 players, 11 rounds				

44...♔b6 45.♘e5 ♘f6 46.♘c4+ ♔c7 47.♘e5 ♘e8 48.♔e6 ♘ed6 49.♘xd6 ♘xd6 50.h4

After the knight swap the white king penetrates decisively. Black is going to lose his kingside pawns.
50...g5 51.h5 ♘b5 52.♔e7 ♘d6 53.g4 ♘b5 54.♔e2 ♘d6 55.♔d3 ♘c8+ 56.♔e6 ♘d6 57.♔f6 ♘d8 58.♔g6

58...♔e7 59.♔xh6 ♔f6 60.♔h7 ♔f7 61.h6 ♘c8 62.♗f5 ♘d6 63.♗e6+

Black resigned.

■ ■ ■

However, the next round brought a major setback for Wang Hao. Against

Levon Aronian he was with his back to the wall from start to finish, but when Aronian failed to deliver the final punch, he could have escaped.

Levon Aronian
Wang Hao
Douglas 2019 (7)

position after 56.♔g5

Wang Hao had been lost earlier on and was fortunate to get to this point. Just one move will hold. 56...♖a3? 57.♖f6 ♖a8 58.♖f5+ ♔e4 59.h5

And Black resigned.
Having seen this, it is possible to deduct the right solution: 56...♖d3! 57.♖f6 ♖d8 58.♖f5+ (58.♖xf3 ♖g8+! is an immediate draw) 58...♔e4 59.h5

ANALYSIS DIAGRAM

NEW! Mega Database 2020*

The ChessBase Mega Database 2020 is the premiere chess database with over 8 million games from 1560 to 2019 in high quality. Packing more than 85,000 annotated games, Mega 2020 contains the world's largest collection of high-class analysed games. Train like a pro! Prepare for your opponents with ChessBase and the Mega Database 2020 and let grandmasters explain how to best handle your favorite variations, improve your repertoire and much more.

- Includes Mega Update Service 2020: update your Mega with your ChessBase 14/15 program every week with over 5,000 new games. That's about 250,000 new games by the end of 2020!
- New, more comfortable design!
- Direct access to the games of all the World Championships, among the over 450 years of chess knowledge.
- Player lexicon for download with over 580,000 player names and more than 40,000 player photos (only with ChessBase 14 or 15)

Mega Database 2020	**€ 189.90**
Update from Mega Database 2019	**€ 69.90**
Update from older Mega Database	**€ 119.90**

Big Database 2020
ChessBase Database without annotation and analysis. 8 million games from 1560 to 2019. No Update Service included.

Big Database 2020	**€ 69.90**

* Available from November 12th

NEW: Corr Database 2020*

The new Corr Database 2020 is the large ChessBase collection of correspondence games from the period from 1804 to 2019. With more than 80,000 tournaments and over 1.6 million correspondence games, the Corr 2020 is a must for all correspondence chess fans. But the Corr Database is very popular even among many grandmasters and trainers, since correspondence games often herald the development of opening theory!

- New, refined layout!
- EXCLUSIVE! Ten selected games from the 29th Correspondence Chess World Championship presented in video analysis by well-known GMs such as Simon Williams, Vidit Gujrathi, Erwin l'Ami, Yannick Pelletier, Mihail Marin, Nihal Sarin and others.
- Let yourself be inspired as chess at the highest level available awaits you!

Corr Database 2020	**€ 189.90**
Update from Corr Database 2018	**€ 99.90**

* Available from November 12th

Online Shop: shop.chessbase.com · ChessBase GmbH · Osterbekstr. 90a · 22083 Hamburg · Germany · info@chessbase.com
CHESSBASE DEALER: NEW IN CHESS · P.O. Box 1093 · NL-1810 KB Alkmaar · phone (+31)72 5127137 · fax (+31)72 5158234 · WWW.NEWINCHESS.COM

59...♖d5!!. And here the difference between the two rook moves on move 56 is clear. Following 60.♖xd5 ♔xd5 61.h6 f2 62.h7 f1♕ 63.h8♕ ♕c1+ the draw becomes obvious.

Levon Aronian played a very fine event, being on the top boards virtually throughout. However, after this victory against Wang Hao he drew his last four games, which proved insufficient to qualify for the Candidates.

Wang Hao continued with a draw against Carlsen and then came very close to defeating Nikita Vitiugov. Once again, the players reached a rook ending, and once again Wang Hao did not get the maximum result out of it.

Nikita Vitiugov
Wang Hao
Douglas 2019 (9)

position after 69.h3

69...♖b3 Much easier is 69...♖f4! 70.♖g3+ ♔f5 71.♖xg5+ ♔xg5 72.♔g3 and now 72...♖g4+ 73.♔xf3 ♖f4+ 74.♔g3 ♖xf2 75.♔xf2 ♔f4 forces a winning pawn ending.
70.♖g3+ ♔f4 71.♖xg5 ♔xg5 72.♔g3

Levon Aronian played a very fine event, but a finish of four draws proved insufficient to qualify for the Candidates Tournament.

72...♖d3
After this move there is no more win for Black. Nor does 72...♔f5 73.♖xf3+ ♖xf3+ 74.♔xf3 ♔e5 75.♔e3 ♔d5 76.♔d3 lead to a win. But 72...♔f6! 73.♖xf3+ (the more stubborn 73.♔f4 loses to 73...♔e6) 73...♖xf3+ 74.♔xf3 ♔f5! leads to a winning pawn ending. But what is actually wrong with the game continuation?
73.♖f1! ♔f5

74.♖e1!
A great defensive effort. The rook on the e-file prevents any winning plan by Black.
74...d5 75.♖e8 ♖c3 76.♖e7 d4 77.♖e8 ♖a3 78.♖e7

Draw agreed. Just try it yourself; there is nothing Black can do.

You can imagine that gaining just one draw out of the two endgames we just looked at would have deeply affected Wang Hao's state of mind, but if so, it certainly didn't show! In Round 10, he defeated Vishy Anand with the black pieces and then in the final Round, 11, this happened.

Caruana looked very strong throughout the event. I was especially impressed by his game against Magnus Carlsen.

**Wang Hao
David Howell**
Douglas 2019 (11)

position after 18.♕a4

If all the games in the final round ended up drawn, Wang Hao would have the best tie-break and would take the Candidates spot. As a consequence, it was logical that the Chinese player didn't want to go for broke, but played a quiet game, weighing his options. His opponent, David Howell, it should be said, had just defeated Bluebaum, Kasimdzhanov and Grischuk before this game and could rightly be called 'on fire'!

I think that after 18...♗e6 the game would probably have ended in a draw, but as Howell mentioned on Twitter after the game, 'his nerves let him down'.

18...♗d5 19.♖d1 Suddenly Black must give up his queen, as otherwise he simply loses a piece.

19...♗xb7 20.♖xd8 ♖xd8 21.f4 ♗xb2 22.♕a7

22...♖d7 22...♖e8 23.♕xb6 ♗g7 is still well within the drawing margins. But the shock of move 18 was probably still resonating.

23.♕xb6 ♗a1 24.♕b5 ♖d1+
24...♗c8! may still hold, but it's agony at this point.
25.♔f2 ♗h1 26.♕e8+ ♔g7

27.♗c5!
Now Black's position collapses.
27...h5 28.♗f8+ ♔f6 29.♕e7+ ♔f5 30.♕xf7+ ♗f6 31.♗e7 ♖d2+ 32.♔e3 ♖xh2 33.♕xf6+ ♔g4 34.♕xg6+ ♔h3 35.f5 ♗d5 36.f6 ♔g2 37.♕c2+

Black resigned.

When 1 and 2 clash
And that's how Wang Hao got to +5 and qualified for the Candidates tournament! He also won the tournament, although he garnered the same number of points as... Fabiano Caruana! Caruana looked very strong throughout the event. I was especially impressed by his game against Magnus Carlsen. The much-anticipated encounter between the number 1 and 2 players in the world happened in Round 9.

**Magnus Carlsen
Fabiano Caruana**
Douglas 2019 (9)
English Opening, Four Knights Variation

1.c4 e5 2.♘c3 ♘f6 3.♘f3 ♘c6 4.e4 ♗c5 5.♘xe5 ♘xe5 6.d4 ♗b4 7.dxe5 ♘xe4

8.♕f3
This move aims to get a favourable version of 8.♕d4 ♘xc3 9.bxc3 ♗e7 10.♕g4 which is the 'old' way of treating this position. With the queen on g3, this position would be much better for White than with the queen on g4. On g4 the queen is vulnerable to an attack by the c8-bishop.
8...♘xc3 9.bxc3

9...♗a5
9...♗e7 10.♕g3 g6 11.♗h6 is known to be very dangerous for Black, ever since Carlsen used it to defeat Anish Giri in the World Blitz Championship. The game continuation is probably stronger, but it took Caruana 20 minutes to make it, because he 'couldn't remember

anything'. It makes the remainder of the game very impressive, since Fabiano seems to navigate the complications with great ease.

10.♗f4

Now 10.♕g3 would be met by 10...♕e7.

10...0-0

11.0-0-0!?

Very enterprising! 11.♗e2 d6 would make life easy for Black.

11...♕e7 12.♔b2 ♖b8 13.♗d3

13...b5!

Opening lines against White's king is both natural and strong. It looks as if White's opening experiment has not borne fruit.

14.cxb5 ♗b7 15.♕h3 g6 16.♕e3

Fabiano Caruana had an imposing 2888 performance. The American tied for first with Wang Hao but had to settle for second place on tiebreak.

16...♖fe8

16...♗d5!? 17.♗g5 ♕e6 is a very interesting continuation. Black's king certainly looks safer than White's. A critical line is 18.♕f4 ♕c6 19.c4 ♗e6 20.♗h6 ♕c5 21.♕f6 ♖xb5+! 22.♔c2 ♕xe5 23.♕xe5 ♖xe5 24.♗xf8 ♔xf8

ANALYSIS DIAGRAM

with fantastic compensation for the exchange. It should be said that Fabiano's move is also perfectly fine. It is generally a good sign for your position if you have various options.

17.♖he1

Played after a long think. Instead, 17.♕xa7 looks scary, and at the very least Black can force a draw with 17...♗xc3+ 18.♔xc3 ♖a8 19.♕xb7 ♕c5+ 20.♗c4 ♖a3+ 21.♔b2 ♕xc4 22.♔xa3 ♕c3+ 23.♔a4 ♕c4+, and perpetual check.

17...♗c6 18.a4 a6 19.♗g5

19...♗xc3+ Fabiano forces the draw. I think Magnus would have done the same after 19...♕f8, with 20.♗h6 ♕e7 21.♗g5, etc. **20.♔xc3 ♕a3+ 21.♔d2 ♕b4+ 22.♔e2 ♕g4+!**

23.♔d2 This had to be foreseen. Now 23.f3 ♕xg2+ is just losing for White, so he is forced to repeat moves. **23...♕b4+ 24.♔e2 ♕g4+ 25.♔d2 ♕b4+** Draw.

A short but lively struggle! ∎

Beyond Material
Ignore the Face Value of Your Pieces and Discover the Importance of Time, Space and Psychology in Chess
Davorin Kuljasevic   336 pages - €22.95

Forget about counting the static value of your pieces, learn the vital skill of taking calculated risks.

"Deserves a wide audience. One of the best books I have read this year."
IM John Donaldson

Side-Stepping Mainline Theory
Cut Down on Opening Study and Get a Middlegame You Are Familiar With
Gerard Welling & Steve Giddins 272 pages - €22.95

"A solid repertoire that could service a club player for many years." – *Mark Haast, Schaaksite*

"I like this book a lot." – *IM Dirk Schuh*

"The authors demonstrate exactly what to aim for in the typical middlegames which arise." – *CHESS Magazine*

An Attacking Repertoire for White with 1.d4
Ambitious Ideas and Powerful Weapons
Victor Moskalenko   368 pages - €29.95

"Crammed full of opening ideas which will suit players of all strengths. His mix of wit, weapons and wisdom strikes me as the ideal source for anyone seeking inspiration."
GM Glenn Flear

"A host of interesting new and dangerous ideas."
John Upham, British Chess News

Forcing Chess Moves
New and Extended 4th Edition
The Key to Better Calculation
Charles Hertan   432 pages - €27.95

New Edition of the award-winning modern classic: 50 extra pages!

"I love this book." – *Elisabeth Vicary, USCF Online*

"When the clock is ticking away, and you have too many viable candidate moves to choose from, remember Hertan's advice." – *Steve Goldberg, ChessCafe*

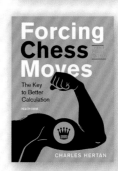

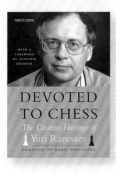

Devoted to Chess
The Creative Heritage of Yuri Razuvaev
Compiled by **Boris Postovsky** 368 pages - €29.95

Yuri Razuvaev (1945-2012) was a leading Soviet GM, a first-rate chess author and a world-class trainer. He worked with Karpov, Kramnik, Gelfand, Lautier, Salov, Topalov, Kosteniuk, Carlsen, Caruana and many others.

"Studying the creative heritage of Yuri Razuvaev will bring you great benefits" – *Vladimir Kramnik*

The Longest Game
The Five Kasparov-Karpov Matches for the World Chess Championship
Jan Timman   304 pages - €29.95

"The ultimate book on Karpov-Kasparov. Monumental."
Johan Hut, Noord Hollands Dagblad

"Makes you wonder: hey, why didn't that book exist before? I couldn't put it down." – *Florian Jacobs, Max Euwe Center*

"You know the outcome, yet you are still glued to your seat, turning the pages." – *Carsten Hansen, ACM*

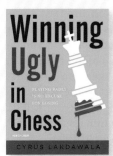

Winning Ugly in Chess
Playing Badly is No Excuse for Losing
Cyrus Lakdawala   336 pages - €22.95

If you rather win a bad game than lose a good one, this is your ideal guide.

"Enjoyable and instructive. Unconditionally recommended."
Thomas Binder, Glarean Magazine

"Lakdawala reminds us that winning is the key goal in chess, not just good moves." – *CHESS Magazine*

The 100 Endgames You Must Know Workbook
Practical Endgames Exercises for Every Chess Player
Jesus de la Villa   288 pages - €22.95

"I love this book! In order to master endgame principles you will need to practice them."
NM Han Schut, Chess.com

"The perfect supplement to De la Villa's manual. To gain sufficient knowledge of theoretical endgames you really only need two books."
IM Herman Grooten, Schaaksite

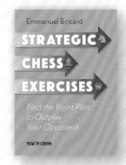

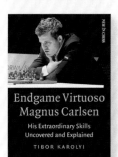

Endgame Virtuoso Magnus Carlsen
His Extraordinary Skills Uncovered and Explained
Tibor Karolyi   272 pages - €24.95

"A real gem! Karolyi manages to entertain and instruct."
GM Karsten Muller, author of 'Fundamental Chess Endings'

"A fantastic book on Carlsen's endgame technique, from which one can learn a great deal." – *IM Dirk Schuh*

"Karolyi has a pleasant style of analysing: objective, not too many variations, with plenty of diagrams. He always ends with useful observations on Carlsen's play."
IM Hans Bohm, De Telegraaf, NL

Strategic Chess Exercises
Find the Right Way to Outplay Your Opponent
Emmanuel Bricard   224 pages - €24.95

Finally an exercises book that is not about tactics!

"Bricard is clearly a very gifted trainer. He selected a superb range of positions and explains the solutions extremely well." – *GM Daniel King*

"For chess coaches this book is nothing short of phenomenal."
Carsten Hansen, author of The Full English Opening

Interview Wang Hao

'I knew that I would have decent chances to win'

Even after he won his first three games, no one saw him as one of the real favourites in the FIDE Grand Swiss in Isle of Man. How could someone seeded 15th finish ahead of virtually the complete elite, including the World Champion? Wang Hao happily explains to **DIRK JAN TEN GEUZENDAM** how he qualified for the Candidates Tournament. And speaks freely about his colleagues and the wondrous worlds of games, anime and manga that fascinate him.

Wang Hao likes speaking his mind. The Chinese grandmaster is eager to express his opinions and give his assessments. You easily get the feeling that he finds it fun to answer questions. Unlike many of his fellow-countrymen, he doesn't smooth his thoughts with careful, diplomatic language, but prefers to say what he thinks. In an almost laconic way, the 30-year-old points out the technical shortcomings of some of his colleagues and tries to look at his own accomplishments in an objective manner.

Answering our first question, he is not going to say that his victory in the Grand Swiss came as a total surprise to him, even though he was only seeded 15th in a colossal field. No,

that's not how it was. 'I thought that I would have very good chances to get some top prize, but nothing else. I was not thinking about first place. I knew that I would have decent chances to win the tournament, but some players, especially those rated 2700+, would have more or less the same chances.

'I didn't do anything special to prepare. Actually, I was helping some of my students in a training camp in China about a week before Isle of Man, which wasn't really useful for myself. I decided to arrive four days before the first round to overcome the jet lag, which was the best preparation, I guess.'

Wang Hao's preparation may not have been optimal, but his start was

explosive. He won his first three games against strong opposition. Esipenko, Mamedov and his compatriot Bu Xiangzhi all bit the dust. It is tempting to suggest that his first-round win against Andrey Esipenko, the young rising star from Russia, must have given him a special boost, but Wang Hao begs to differ.

'It was totally expected that I could win the first round with White. It was clear that my young opponent, while good at opening preparation, has some weaknesses, especially his positional understanding is not very strong. Beating him didn't mean very much; it was too early to say anything. But I was very fortunate to win three games in a row, as these opponents are generally very difficult to beat. I thought that

MARIA EMELIANOVA

Wang Hao: 'I only like to check ideas with engines and don't like solving puzzles at all.'

I had an excellent start, beyond my expectations.'

With 11 rounds, it was a very long competition, in which finding the right rhythm is of great importance. What was your daily routine?

'Before most of my games I spent about one hour on preparation, which was probably enough, since I needed the energy during the game more. In fact, I had trouble sleeping, and since I couldn't sleep, I spent a lot of time with the game *Fire Emblem: Three Houses* on my Nintendo Switch.

'As for the social life, after breakfast I would go for a walk, for about 40 minutes to an hour, with my good friend Mircea Parligras. Sometimes Constantin Lupulescu and Bassem Amin also joined, because all of us shared the same table at breakfast almost every day. And in the evening, I usually went to the city centre of Douglas for dinner with friends. A couple of times I also went for a walk with my good friend Peter Leko. We

'Since I couldn't sleep, I spent a lot of time with the game *Fire Emblem: Three Houses* on my Nintendo Switch.'

enjoyed the wind of the seaside. The night before the last day, we even saw a starry sky when we were on the way back to the hotel. It was really amazing.'

After a solid draw with Caruana you made a highly entertaining draw with Maghsoodloo. Great stuff for the audience. Were you enjoying yourself?
'Well, that game was full of mistakes, an up-and-down game. I can't say that I was enjoying it, because I could easily have lost before the first time-control. It was only because my opponent was trying to play for time and made terrible moves that I managed to get chances. Actually, after the game we both agreed that it would have been better if the game had ended peacefully much quicker, because it wasn't good for our hearts.'

And then in Round 7 your luck seemed to run out, as you lost to your old friend Aronian. That must have been tough, as you seemed to be close to a draw.
'Yeah, the rook ending was totally drawish. I was really tired after a long time defending, and I missed a few simple ways to draw the position. Even at the very last moment I could still make a draw, but that one required very precise calculation and I was low on time and very tired. After the game I felt extremely dizzy, because I simply had no energy left.'

Next you made a solid draw against Carlsen. Did you want to avoid any risk in that game?
'I was really exhausted after the game

'I feel attracted to these worlds of fiction, because I really think that my own life is not interesting enough.'

with Levon (Aronian). Peter (Leko) suggested I make a solid draw with White, and I also thought that would be a good idea. To save energy and avoid any risk.'

In Round 9, you pressed against Vitiugov and could have won. How disappointing was that missed opportunity?
'I was disappointed that I spent too much energy in that game and that it was too long. Nikita played not so well in an equal position, and I could very slowly improve my position. Once you get into time-trouble with little energy, anything can happen. In fact, I would have been very happy if he had chosen to repeat somewhere before move 30, when the position was still equal. I could happily have gone to a restaurant in the city. In the end, the punishment was that I missed dinner.'

And then you won your last two games; very impressive. In a way it reminded me of Norway Chess 2013, when you beat Carlsen and Anand in the final two rounds. Is the similarity a coincidence, or do you feel you have the strength for such strong finishes?
'Of course, no one can win such a strong Swiss tournament without any luck. I guess that it was just a coincidence. I was ready to play for a draw with Vishy (Anand) and wait for a better chance in the last round. Of course no one, including myself, could have expected Vishy to collapse that quickly with White. After Round 10, I suddenly found myself in a position in which I had the best chances, both for being the champion and for qualifying for the Candidates tournament. I am pleased that I took that chance.'

Who do you feel will be your biggest rivals in the Candidates tournament?
'I don't know. All the players will have decent chances, but I think that Fabiano (Caruana) will probably have the best preparation.'

You did not play on the Chinese team during the last few Olympiads. Will you have support from other Chinese players?
'I am good friends with most of the young players in China, and some of them will help me to prepare for the Candidates tournament.'

Your main experience with the Candidates so far was training with Levon Aronian when he prepared for the 2011 Candidates matches. What did you learn from that experience?
'I had a great time during that training camp and I really enjoyed the conversations with Levon (Aronian), Gabriel (Sargissian) and Hrant [Akobian – Aronian's manager – DJtG]. But it was almost nine years ago, and I am not so sure that it is still a useful experience for the Candidates tournament next year. Levon probably already changed a lot in his approach, as back then the engines were not as strong as they are today. Also, Levon's way of training and mine were significantly different. (With a smile) I always liked my way. Levon preferred to analyse more on the board and he likes solving puzzles. I only like to check ideas with engines and I don't like solving puzzles at all.'

In the past years you have been less active as a competitive player. Were there other things you were doing that were chess related?
'Yes, I started coaching some players, which took a lot of my time. But my students are good players. I could still improve myself by coaching them. We have both Internet and face-to-face sessions. In the first case, we can be anywhere with a good connection, but if we want to really meet, my students usually come to my home in Beijing.'

You have always taken a broad interest in life outside of chess. What other things keep you occupied?
'I love travelling a lot, to discover new, interesting and attractive places for the fun of it. I also like finding good restaurants to try different types of delicious food. But since my stomach has become sensitive because of the stress, I have to try to control myself. And I am a big fan of anime, games and reading, and I really enjoy myself when I can immerse myself in my hobbies.'

I have the feeling that your favourites are little known to many of our readers. Could you give some tips or suggestions?
'I have watched a lot of anime. My all-time favourite movies are *Princess Mononoke* and *Spirited Away*, both directed by Miyazaki Hayao, and *Paprika*, directed by Kon Satoshi.

'Actually, I also read a lot of manga. My favourite series is *Jojo's Bizarre Adventure*, written by Araki Hirohiko, especial part 7, *The Steel Balls Run*.

'As for games, although originally I started out playing strategic games, such as the Romance of Three Kingdoms Series, now most of my favourite games are RPG, role-playing games. Some four years ago, I was really addicted to *The Witcher 3: Wild Hunt*. I am also a big fan of *Persona 5, Nier: Automata*.

'I feel attracted to these worlds of fiction, because I really want to experience much more than my own life. I don't really think that my life is interesting enough, and by watching or reading or playing all this, no matter if it's fantasy or based on real life, I get to know more stories, which fulfils my life.' ∎

Great 2019 titles from Quality Chess

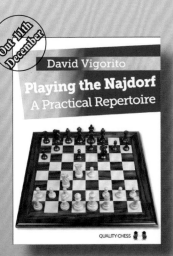

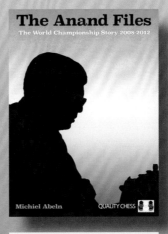
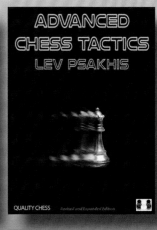

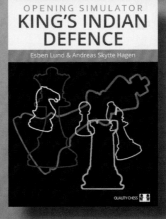
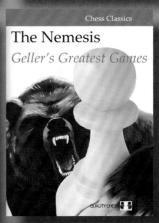

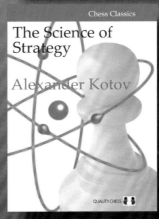
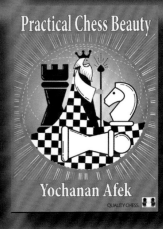

MAXIMize your Tactics

with Maxim Notkin

Find the best move in the positions below

Solutions on page 75

1. White to play

2. White to play

3. White to play

4. White to play

5. Black to play

6. White to play

7. Black to play

8. Black to play

9. White to play

GIBRALTAR
INTERNATIONAL CHESS FESTIVAL
20th to 31st January 2020   www.gibchess.com

Bringing people together since 2003

#gibchess

For more information on our **UNIVERSITY CHESS SEMINAR** 16th to 18th JANUARY 2020 and our **GIBRALTAR INTERNATIONAL CHESS FESTIVAL** 20th to 31st JANUARY 2020

please email **chess@caletahotel.gi**

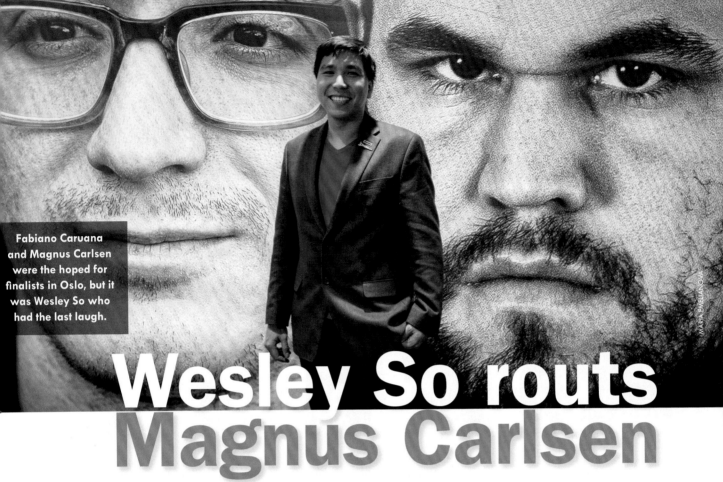

Fabiano Caruana and Magnus Carlsen were the hoped for finalists in Oslo, but it was Wesley So who had the last laugh.

Wesley So routs Magnus Carlsen

American is the first Fischer Random World Champion

The first official Fischer Random World Championship took place in Oslo. Magnus Carlsen was the hot favourite, but the local hero stood no chance in the final, in which Wesley So was merciless. After four wins for the American and two draws the title was his.

This official championship, sanctioned by FIDE, was a logical sequel to the inaugural 'unofficial' championship that was staged by the same Norwegian organizers last year. That match, without a qualification process, between Magnus Carlsen and Hikaru Nakamura, was won by the classical World Champion. Nakamura had been invited because in 2009 he had been the last winner of the Chess960 championship in Mainz, which was for many

years the main promoter of Bobby Fischer's brainchild.

The match between Carlsen and Nakamura had been a great success. Close to two million Norwegians followed the final on television, a stunning number, given the total population of 5.3 million, and especially because the Winter Olympics, which can always count on enormous interest in Norway, were being held at the same time.

This time, all eyes were obviously on Magnus Carlsen again, and he seemed to be on schedule when he

disposed of the world's number two Fabiano Caruana in the semi-final. For Wesley So, the route to the final had been less smooth. To begin with, he had to qualify for the semi-finals and finals in Oslo in the preliminaries, which were organized online by chess.com. There he lost his encounter with Hikaru Nakamura, 3-9, but profited from the rule that allowed a backdoor for the losers at that stage. Grabbing that opportunity, he defeated Peter Svidler 6½-5½ and earned a spot in the semi-final in Norway.

His semi-final match against Ian Nepomniachtchi was an eventful clash, in which So managed his nerves best and won convincingly 31-5. Each match consisted of games with different time-controls. The players started with four 'slow rapid games' in which a win yielded three points, followed by four 'fast rapid games' in which a win was worth two points. Next blitz games were scheduled, where a win yielded the winner one point. Each match was decided once a player had collected 12½ points. This meant that Wesley So's mission had been accomplished before the blitz games, both against Nepomniachtchi and against Carlsen!

Establishing new theory

Most top players are fond of Fischer Random chess. One reason often mentioned is that they are freed of the burden to remember loads of theory. For this championship, a new position was selected every day, which was used for all games on that day. Needless to say, chess players will be chess players, and in the course of each day they tried to establish an initial amount of theory about the position under discussion.

A key game from the final between Magnus Carlsen and Wesley So was the second 'slow rapid game', which ended in the American's first win. Here it is, with notes by the champion.

NOTES BY
Wesley So

Wesley So
Magnus Carlsen
Oslo 2019 (2nd match game)
Winning the FIDE World Fischer Random Chess Championship was a huge deal for me, partly because it was completely unexpected. Despite an overcrowded year of commitments, when approached to be part of this new kind of tournament,

'I love Chess960. You become an artist with a new box of never-before-seen colours to paint with.'

I accepted because I love Chess960. You become an artist with a new box of never-before-seen colours to paint with.

I had no real thought of actually winning. I just wanted to play some fun chess. I'd only played 960 seriously a couple of times in the last two years, both over the board in St. Louis.

For this event, I had to endure a long online knock-out process. Due to a heavy travel schedule, the matches were stuck in whenever they fitted between my obligations. In the inevitable chaos, I played every match thinking it would be my last, and in the quarter-finals it almost was. I had just returned from Khanty-Mansiysk with jet lag and a horrible cold. I lost my match.

Given a chance to redeem myself, I pushed through and was shocked when I realized I had actually made it to the semi-finals in Norway! Okay, so it had to be squeezed in between the Isle of Man Swiss and a Grand Chess Tour leg in Romania, I would again be tired and unprepared, but even last place was a good payday, and who doesn't love Norway?

No one could have made up the end of this story. Certainly not me. I got through the semi-finals but still... Magnus Carlsen had roasted Fabiano Caruana, who had roasted the great Garry Kasparov (in a recent Fischer Random match in St. Louis not connected with this championship –ed.). OK... second place wouldn't be so horrible. Plus the chess had been exciting fun. But then... what can I say? My God is the maker of miracles!

starting position

This is the second game with a very interesting starting position. We have a normal-looking chess position, except the queens are in the corner. All chess players will agree that the corner is one of the worst spots for the queen. A queen on a1/a8 needs to be activated soon, otherwise we could run into the real trouble of being out of play. Controlling or occupying the centre in the opening is nice, so in my few minutes of preparation before the game, I checked all kinds of moves: 1.e4, 1.d4, 1.c4, 1.♘g3 and even 1.b3.

1.d4

In the first game of the final, Magnus Carlsen played 1.c4, when I should

What is Fischer Random Chess?

Fischer Random, or Chess 960, was invented by the 11th World Champion, Bobby Fischer. To reduce the importance of opening theory, in the starting position, the pieces on each player's back rank are randomly shuffled. But not every random position is allowed: the two bishops must be on opposite colours, and the kings must be between the rooks, so they can castle both ways.

For the rest, the normal chess rules apply. This also goes for castling, one thing you have to get used to in Fischer Random. Both the king and the rook must not have moved yet, the king cannot be in check, and cannot cross a square that is under check. After castling the king and rook end up on the traditional squares of standard chess. So, castling kingside ends with the king on f1 and the rook on f1. To give an example: even if before castling the king is on b1 and the rook on e1, after castling kingside, they will find themselves on g1 and f1.

A fascinating move. This reminds us of the Queen's Indian, but without the pawn on c4 and with the queen on a8!

have replied 1...c5. Instead, I went 1...e6 (in my White game I didn't go for 1.c4, as the position after 1...c5 2.♘c3 ♘c6 3.e3 e6 4.d4 cxd4 5.exd4 d5 6.cxd5 exd5 7.♘g3 seems a little too symmetrical to me: 7...♘g6 8.♗d3 ♗d6. All these moves here seem very logical, and it is hard to imagine White being able to use the extra tempo to much good use) 2.♘c3 d5 3.d4 dxc4 4.e3 a6 5.a4 b6 6.♗xc4 ♗b7 7.♕b1! ♘g6 8.e4 ♗b4 9.♘g3

and White is better because of his central control and my badly placed queen on a8. Later Magnus put a lot of pressure on me, but I managed to survive after having to go through some tense moments. He missed a clear win, and then I somehow managed to escape and save a pawn-down endgame with drawing chances.

1.e4 c5 did not appeal to me. After a normal continuation, 2.d4 cxd4 3.♖xd4 ♘c6 4.♖d1, we get a normal-looking Sicilian position, in which the 960 position favours Black. White lost his castling rights, and the queen on a1 looks silly.

1...b6

I had not expected this, and had mostly analysed 1...d5. But it makes total sense to activate the queen asap.

2.♘g3

Threatening 3.e4.

2...♗a6!?

A fascinating move. This reminds us of the Queen's Indian, but without the pawn on c4 and with the queen on a8! Needless to say, I do not want to lose my castling rights, so I did not even bother considering 3.e4.

Maybe Magnus did not like 2...d5, which could be met by 3.c4 dxc4 4.e3.

3.b3

As in the good old modern days, I decided to firmly protect the c4-square with a pawn. White has a stronger move, though.

White could fight for more with 3.d5! e6 4.e4 ♗xf1 5.♘xf1, when he does not forfeit his castling rights and controls a lot of space on the board.

3...e6

I was planning to meet 3...d5 with 4.♗a3 ♘g6, and here we get a symmetrical position again. I can play ♘d2 or e3, with some hopes to use my first-move advantage.

4.c4 d5 5.e3

5...♗e7 Quite perplexing.

I do not see any difference between this and 5...♘g6, so perhaps Magnus just wanted to be fancy and move the bishop first.

6.♘c3 ♘g6 7.♗d3

Just developing and getting a normal position. It's clear that both sides could be quite satisfied with how the opening turned out. White has some space advantage on the queenside, while Black has managed to develop and control a fair amount of squares in the centre. Black has a decent QID position. Obviously I could have gained a strong initiative on move 3, but I missed my chance.

7...0-0 8.0-0 ♘d7

9.cxd5?!

I thought I was getting a good and solid Queen's Gambit Declined structure, but in fact only Black can be fine here.

I saw 9.♘b5!, which is in fact the strongest move: 9...♗xb5 (9...♕b8 10.cxd5 exd5 11.♕c3) 10.cxb5 c6, when it does not seem to me White has much. But the bishop pair could, in fact, be quite annoying: 11.bxc6 ♕xc6 12.♕b2 (12.♘h5 is good, too) 12...♘f6 13.♕e2, when Black has problems in view of his weak light squares on the queenside.

9.♘b5 was my last chance to have some opening advantage.

9.♕b2 c6 10.♕e2 f5 looks like a good Stonewall for Black.

9...♗xd3 10.♖xd3 exd5 11.♘f5

I thought this pawn structure slightly favoured White, but in fact Black is totally fine. My main problem is the bishop on c1, I think, which looks slightly passive.

11.a4!?, with the idea of ♗a3, might be an option. Either way Black is totally fine.

11...♖fe8 12.♘xe7+ ♖xe7

13.b4?!

The idea to push pawns on the queen-side is tempting, but in reality I do not have enough time for this. The tempo is better spent improving the position of my pieces.

In hindsight, a move like 13.f3 ♘f6 14.♘e2 would have been better. White does not have any weaknesses and has a flexible position.

Or 13.♘e2, with the idea of doubling on the c-file.

13...♘f6 14.b5 c6

14...c5!? was also interesting.

15.a4 15.bxc6 ♕xc6 only hands Black the open c-file.

15...h5

16.h3

My first intention of 16.a5 would have run into 16...cxb5 17.♘xb5 (17.axb6? b4) 17...♕c6, when it seems that White has to fight for equality.

16...♕c8 17.bxc6 ♖e6

Here I was not very pleased with my position. Black controls the open c-file, his knights could possibly threaten my king, and my rook on d3 looks funny. After thinking for a

while I realized that I could not fight for control of the c-file. Having no other choice, I decided to open up the centre.

18.f3

18...♖xc6

I was expecting 18...♕xc6, which prevents e4, but I can play 19.♗d2 ♖c8 20.♕b1, with an unclear game. White should not be worse.

19.e4 dxe4

19...♕d7 is fine, but Black has to find 20.♗g5 ♖e8! 21.♗xf6 ♘f4!, which I doubt any player would.

Four semi-finalists ready for the final stage of the Fischer Random World Championship: Ian Nepomniachtchi, Magnus Carlsen, Fabiano Caruana and Wesley So.

MARIA EMELIANOVA

20.fxe4

20...♘e5!?

Magnus played this confidently. However, he must have missed something in his calculations, since only White could be better later.

20...♕a6 was what I had expected: 21.♖fd1 ♖dc8, with a very lopsided game. My pawns control a lot of squares in the centre, but at the same time they are vulnerable.

20...♖d7!? is a very deep prophylactic move. Now ♗g5 won't be a pin. 21.♗b2 ♖e6 (21...♖c4 is also complex) 22.♖e1 ♖e8 23.♕d1 ♕d8, and again both sides have an interesting and playable position. If I had to choose which side to take, I'd probably take White's centre, but to make progress is far from easy.

20...♖c4? 21.♗g5 pins his knight.

21.♖e3

21...♘c4

Since 21...♖xd4 is met by 22.♘e2, I am safe for the time being.

22.♖ef3

After thinking for a while I initiate complications. The position does not look at all clear to me at this point.

22.♖d3 ♘e5 is a repetition, and

As Wesley So receives the winner's trophy from the president of the Norwegian Chess Federation Morten Madsen, Magnus Carlsen shows how happy he is with second place.

after 22.♖ee1 ♘a5 23.♘b5 ♘b3 the position is equal.

22...♖xd4 23.♘d5 ♖xe4

24.♗h6!?

Objectively mediocre, but it looked so tempting to me that I just had to play it against Magnus. And I suppose you also have to be a computer to find/calculate all the best variations to the end.

Of course my first intention was 24.♖xf6. But it leads to a simple draw if he finds the right defence: 24...gxf6 25.♘xf6+ ♖xf6 26.♕xf6 ♕c5+! (this is even simpler than 26...♕e6

27.♕g5+ ♕g6 28.♕d8+ ♔g7 29.♗g5 ♖e6 30.♗e7 ♘e5 31.♔h2, when in view of his more exposed king Black has some trouble) 27.♔h1 ♕e7 28.♕f3 h4, when it should end in a draw, because Black's king is too vulnerable.

24...♘e8

People later opined that 24...♕d7! would be a refutation; but even then Black would still be fighting for equality: 25.♖g3 ♕xd5 26.♖xf6 ♕e5 (26...♖xf6 27.♕xf6 ♕d4+ 28.♕xd4 ♖xd4 29.♖xg7+ ♔h8 30.♖xf7 a6 should also be a draw).

ANALYSIS DIAGRAM

It looks as if Black is better, but after 27.♖xg7+ ♔h8 28.♕xe5 ♘xe5 29.♖xc6 ♘xc6 30.♖xf7 White's activity is enough for the draw, e.g. 30...♖xa4 31.♖c7 ♖c4 32.♔f2 (intending g4-g5) 32...h4 33.g4 hxg3+ 34.♔xg3 b5 35.h4, and this should be a draw.

25.♗xg7

25...♘d2 The only move. For a moment I thought I was lost (rook down), but then I spotted 28.♗e5. Instead, 25...♘xg7 26.♖xf7 ♖g6 27.♖xg7+ ♖xg7 28.♘f6+ ♔h8 29.♘xe4 just crushes Black.

26.♖xf7 ♘xf1 27.♖f8+ ♔h7

28.♗e5! An incredible attack! I am a full rook down and also have back rank problems, but thanks to the weird placement of Black's pieces I can regain my sacrificed material.

28...♖c1 I was expecting 28...♕e6 29.♖h8+ ♔g6 30.♘f4+ ♖xf4 31.♗xf4, when Black has to be careful, but he should hold after 31...♘f6 (31...♕e4? 32.♖g8+ ♔f7 33.♕h8! leads to an irresistible attack) 32.♕xf1 ♕d5!.

29.♖h8+ ♔g6 30.♘e7+ ♔f7

31.♖h7+ A tricky little check. After 31.♕a2+ ♕c4 (31...♔e7 32.♖h7+, and mate soon) 32.♕f2+ Black saves himself with 32...♖f4! (32...♔e7 33.♕f8 is mate in eight, according to the computer) 33.♗xf4 ♘e3+ 34.♔h2 ♘f1+ 35.♔g1, with a draw. An incredible line!

31...♔e6?!

This make the defence trickier. 31...♔f8 32.♘xc8 ♖xa1 33.♗xa1 ♘g3 34.♔f2 ♖xa4 should be an easy draw.

32.♘xc8 ♖xa1 33.♗xa1 ♘g3 34.♖xa7 Check first, 34.♖e7+ might be more accurate. I'm not sure why.

34...♘f5 35.♗h8! I like this move; it shows the true power of the bishop.

35...♖e2?

A huge blunder. This immediately loses the game. Magnus must have been pressured for time just as we are closing in on the time-control.

Basically any logical move should be enough for a draw, e.g. 35...♖e1+ 36.♔f2 ♖c1 37.♘xb6 ♖c2+ 38.♔e1 ♖xg2 39.a5 ♘ed6, when Black's activity is enough. The White king is too passive on the back rank.

36.g4 hxg4 37.hxg4

37...♘e3 There is no longer any way to save the game. 37...♔g3 38.♖e7+ leads to an easy endgame, e.g. 38...♔d5 39.♘xb6+ ♔c6 40.♖xe2 ♘xe2+ 41.♔f2 ♔xb6 42.♔xe2 ♔a5 43.♔d3! ♔xa4 44.♔c4! (shouldering away the Black king and winning) 44...♔a5 45.♔c5!.

38.♖e7+ ♔d5 39.♖xe8

It's not often that you can pick up a free piece against Magnus.

39...♔g2+ 40.♔h1 ♖xg4 41.♖xe3

41.♘xb6+ ♔c6 42.a5 wins easily as well, but I decided to rid him of a pesky knight.

41...♖h4+ 42.♔g2 ♖xh8 43.♘xb6+ ♔c5 44.♖b3 ♖h4

45.♖b5+ Here 45.a5! was simpler, and I saw it but I decided not to rush: 45...♖h7 (45...♖h6 46.♘d7+ ♔d4 47.♖b6) 46.♘c8 (46.a6 ♖a7 47.♘a4+, followed by 48.♖b6, wins easily as well, since his king will be unable to approach the a6-pawn) 46...♖h6 47.♖b6, and White wins.

45...♔c6 46.♖b1 ♖h5

Threatening ...♖a5-a6, with a draw!

47.♘c4 47.♔g3? ♖a5! was his last trick: 48.♔f4 (48.♖b4 ♔c5) 48...♖a6, with a draw.

47...♖h4 48.♘b6 ♖h5 49.♘c4 ♖h4

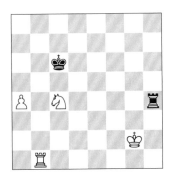

50.♘b2

This looks passive, but my king walks over to the queenside with enough time. Also, with the knight behind the passed pawn, it ensures that all pawn endings are winning for me.

50...♔b6 51.♔g3 ♖d4 Or 51...♖h8 52.♔f3 ♔a5 53.♖g1, winning.

52.♔f3 ♔a5 53.♔e3

Oslo 2019

	slow rapid	fast rapid	total
Semi-Finals			
Nepomniachtchi-So	3-9	2-4	5-13
Carlsen-Caruana	7½-4½	5-3	12½-7½
Final			
Carlsen-So	1½-10½	1-3	2½-13½

(details on the scoring system are given in the report)

Even on my flight out, the Norwegian flight attendants took the time to announce that there was a World Chess Champion on board (kind of embarrassing actually).

53...♖d8 If 53...♖h4 then 54.♖g1 ♔b4 55.♖g5 ♔a3 56.♖b5, and wins.

54.♖h1 ♖d5 55.♖h4 ♖g5 56.♔d3 ♖c5 57.♖c4 ♖h5 58.♔c2 ♖h3 59.♖c3 ♖h6 60.♔b3 ♖b6+ 61.♔a3 ♖c6

62.♖c4

Fedoseev had tried a similar stalemate trick against me in the online 960 quarter-finals a few weeks before (I had a bishop and rook against his lone bishop), so I was very familiar with such ideas!

62...♖h6 63.♖c5+ ♔a6 64.♔b4 ♖h1 65.♖c6+

65...♔a7 Or 65...♔b7 66.♔b5 ♖b1 67.♖c2 ♔a7 68.a5 ♔b7 69.a6+ ♔a7 70.♔a5, and 71.♘a4. **66.♘c4 ♔b7 67.♖b6+ ♔a7 68.♖g6 ♖b1+ 69.♔a5 ♖h1 70.♖g7+ ♔b8 71.♖a6 ♖h5 72.♖g8+**

Black resigned.

This was a huge win for me. I was very satisfied to have saved the first game and to have won this one after not getting anything out of the opening.

I want to give credit to the Norwegian sense of fair play. I was aware that I had caused national pain, yet Norwegians everywhere did not hesitate to warmly congratulate me. Even on my flight out, the Norwegian flight attendants took the time to announce that there was a World Chess Champion on board (kind of embarrassing actually). Thank you to Dund/AS and chess.com for their generous sponsorship and management of this event. Thank you to FIDE President Dvorkovich for his vision for chess. Thank you to Norway and its very fine people.

P.S. My love of Fischer Random turned out to be infectious and I'm currently collaborating with Chessable on a video instruction course on Fischer Random strategy and tactics. ■

James Mortimer: 'To those who have taken up chess as an intellectual and fascinating pastime, and who are often beaten at odds by players of inferior grammar, it will be cheering to know that many persons are skilful chessplayers, though in some instances their brains, in a general way, compare unfavourably with the cogitative faculties of a rabbit.' *(The American chess player, journalist, and playwright (1832-1911); one of the few who witnessed the famous Anderssen-Morphy match)*

Magnus Carlsen: 'The streak was nice but the performance was mediocre.' *(Interviewed at the end of the FIDE Grand Swiss in the Isle of Man, after passing Ding Liren's elite-level unbeaten streak of 100 games)*

Sergei Tiviakov: 'Real chess players know that I have the record!' *(The Russian-Dutch GM interviewed by the Norwegian newspaper Aftenpost, on the World Champion passing Ding Liren's record)*

Espen Agdestein: 'Magnus is in super-heavy-weight, while Tiviakov is middleweight.' *(The World Champion's manager responding to Tiviakov in Aftenpost)*

Ulf Andersson: 'All my losses are bitter. It is normal to suffer when it is going bad! There is nothing new about that, I believe. I suppose all players suffer when they lose. I suppose, when you put your heart in something and when it does not go how you wish, then you suffer.' *(Interviewed during the 2009 Magistral Casino de Barcelona)*

Barbra Streisand: 'You know who I had a crush on when I was in school? Bobby Fischer. He was a year younger than me, but I would have lunch with him every day and he would sit there, laughing hysterically, reading *Mad* magazine. Right? And he wore these earlaps on his ears. He was always alone and very peculiar. But I found him very sexy. I was 16 and he was 15.' *(The film/song diva, interviewed for Playboy, October 1977)*

Jason Statham: 'Chess is like the art of war on 64 squares. It's a killer game. You're only as good as your opponent.' *(The English Hollywood action hero on his longstanding chess rivalry with film director Guy Ritchie, which was renewed in October with a series of Instagram pictures of the two battling over the board)*

Alexander Beliavsky: 'Chess is a very easy game; all you need to do is calculate lines, and everything will be okay.'

Jon Speelman: 'The initial position is decisive zugzwang!'

Vladimir Kramnik: 'Mikhail Tal was a star; a genuine chess genius. As far as I understand, this man was completely devoid of ambition and played chess primarily for his pleasure – he delighted in the game. This approach is absolutely not professional. But his talent was so improbable that even with such an approach, being in the sense a chess amateur, Tal became World Champion.' *(In a 2004 interview with Vladimir Barsky published on e3e5.com)*

Wolfgang Heidenfeld: 'Chess is a difficult game. If it were less difficult it would not be so much fun.' *(In his 1970 book Lacking the Master Touch)*

Baadur Jobava: 'I have lost five years of my living life by playing these crazy games.' *(After playing a fantastic game to beat David Howell in the Isle of Man)*

G.H. Hardy: 'The "great game" of chess is primarily psychological, a conflict between one trained intelligence and another, and not a mere collection of small mathematical theorems.' *(The chess-loving English mathematician (1877-1947), known for his achievements in number theory and mathematical analysis, writing in his book 'A Mathematician's Apology')*

Boris Gelfand: 'The good thing in chess is that very often the best moves are the most beautiful ones. The beauty of logic.'

The Moves that Matter

A Chess Grandmaster on the Game of Life

In the summer of 2008, **JONATHAN ROWSON** helped Vishy Anand prepare for his World Championship match against Vladimir Kramnik. In a fragment from his new book *The Moves that Matter*, Rowson remembers how he was confounded by the question how many cores his laptop had. 'I will never forget that feeling of being an analogue creature, floundering in a digital world.'

There is a story of Mahatma Gandhi boarding a train that had just started to pick up speed. When one of his sandals fell off in the process of embarking, he instinctively removed the other one and threw it down, so that somebody else would find them, and have a pair to wear. No despair at the loss, no befuddlement, just a clear action grounded in compassion for a person in need whom he had not yet met. Many of us might see the wisdom in the act, but only several moments later when it would be too late.

My Ph.D. thesis was a sustained reflection on what we can learn from that kind of story, of which there are many. The aim was to consider wisdom not as a folksy construct relating to sage advice, but rather to try to understand how we might better become ready, willing and able to help others in complex or charged situations.

Most doctorates have a clear, narrow and specific research question within a single discipline, but I had no appetite for that. Through chess I had already tasted domain-specific expertise and shared it widely in writing; and what I really wanted to understand was the broad transdisciplinary question of what it means to become wiser.

The thesis involved lots of reading and conceptual wrestling, and trying to make sense – partly through my own meditation efforts – of what exactly is supposed to transform through spiritual practice. In the end my examiners were satisfied. My main supervisor, Professor Guy Claxton, remarked that while he had hoped my thesis would become more like a carefully curated wedding cake, he was happy that I had produced such a delicious bowl of spaghetti.

In the summer of 2008, I was a few months from finishing the thesis. As fellow doctoral survivors will know, it's not easy to write between 80,000 and 100,000 coherent words that represent something resembling a contribution to knowledge. But I was in the home straight, and had set 5 November 2008 as my delivery date, partly because this was the day Barack Obama was expected to be elected the first African American president. I figured if I was going to be distracted by the political drama

The scene was like a Silicon Valley incubator house: humanoids with transfixed faces lit by the glow of computer screens.

I expected the training to be roughly 20 per cent physical, 20 per cent psychological, 30 per cent joint analysis over the board and 30 per cent on the computer. In fact, the work was about 95 per cent on the computer.

of the time – which I was – I should also be motivated by it. I was not yet aware that I would be a father the following year, but it was in that life context of beginning to detach from the chess world that I had the privilege of helping world champion Viswanathan Anand prepare for his match with Vladimir Kramnik.

Kramnik is figuratively and literally a Russian giant who dethroned Garry Kasparov after his twenty years at the top. Anand won the official World Championship in a tournament format around the same time, but years of tedious chess politics meant that these two players had never met in a match. When it became clear that the chess world was going to get the contest it wanted, I offered my services to Anand. I was a strong middleweight Grandmaster rather than a heavyweight, but analytical help is about more than chess strength. Unlike many hired guns, I had some lateral perspectives on chess, an easy rapport with Vishy, and I genuinely wanted him to win. The plan was to offer a few opening ideas for him to develop and some speculative psychological insight for him to ignore.

I was also eager to participate in preparation at the very highest level. I had no experience of World Championship preparation, but I had read descriptions of other matches from the seventies, eighties and nineties. Most of those matches were in pre-computer or early computer days, and what I assumed might be a slight shift in emphasis was much more fundamental. I imagined that the training would be part over-the-board analysis session, part inquiry into the psychodynamics of competition, and part *Rocky IV* training montage, where Sylvester Stallone lifts huge blocks of wood and runs through the snow. I expected the training to be roughly 20 per cent physical, 20 per cent psychological, 30 per cent joint analysis over the board and 30 per cent on the computer.

In fact, the work was about 95 per cent on the computer, and virtually all of that time was spent trying to help Vishy form new ways of achieving good positions in the opening phase of the game. Just as finding a needle in a haystack is easy, if you have a metal detector, finding an important new chess move is easy, if you have the right software. Analysis engines can give an immediate numerical assessment of what is happening in a position, including which move is best, who is better placed and by how much. These engines are our guide, and Grandmasters are like knowledgeable and eager tourists, asking informed questions to yield unconventional insight.

The camp, as chess players call their training venues, was Vishy's main European base, a smallish two-bedroom apartment just outside Frankfurt in Germany. The only sign of chess as such was a half-forgotten set on a coffee table near the window. I was accompanied by the Danish Grandmaster Peter Heine Nielsen – Vishy's long-term adviser, now working for Magnus Carlsen, and the former FIDE world champion Rustam Kasimdzhanov, who hails from Uzbekistan but had been resident in Germany for several years. The three of us got on well and stayed at a nearby hotel.

In general the morale of the group was high, and during breaks we watched comedy clips on YouTube. On most days there was a group jog in the morning including some steep stairs, but it was a little ad hoc, and then there were some musings about

Jonathan Rowson (1977) is a writer, philosopher and chess grandmaster, who was British Chess Champion from 2004-2006. He holds degrees from Oxford, Bristol and Harvard universities, was formerly Director of the Social Brain Centre at the RSA and an Open Society Fellow. He is co-founder and director of Perspectiva, a research institute that examines the relationships between complex global challenges and the inner lives of human beings.

In chess circles, Rowson is probably best known as the author of the modern classics *The Seven Deadly Chess Sins* (2000) and *Chess for Zebras* (2005). His new book, *The Moves that Matter*, is not a chess book, although it is clear from the subtitle, *A Chess Grandmaster on the Game of Life*, that chess plays a prominent role in the sociological and philosophical ideas that he expounds.

Preparing with a world champion for a World Championship match was precious to me not because it was extraordinary but because it was mundane.

match strategy over lunch, which we usually ate in a Thai restaurant about ten minutes away. *The work* however, happened as the four of us sat around the same table in our own worlds for several hours in a dimly lit room late into the night. The scene was like a Silicon Valley incubator house: humanoids with transfixed faces lit by the glow of computer screens. Onlookers would not have been able to guess what we were doing in that room.

We typically listened to Coldplay from Peter's computer, a benign cheering hum with occasional blasts of euphoria, which grew on me. I introduced the Israeli vocalist Yael Naim to Kasim's delight, though Vishy protested when I tried to play Tracy Chapman for the second time. I made just enough warm drinks for the team to remind ourselves we had bodies, but stopped short of being a *chaiwala*. I noticed that at the end of each day Vishy would eagerly go to the kitchen to clean up and thereby unwind from the chess and his computer screen, which I came to realise were more or less the same thing for him.

Mostly we followed the best ideas according to the analysis engines with what Vishy joked was 'space-bar preparation' – when the analysis engines are synchronised with the position you are navigating, rather than move the pieces on the screen with your mouse, you press the space bar to keep the engine going down the line it deems to be most accurate for both sides, while watching it unfold on the position on the screen. It is a kind of thinking, I suppose.

You do pause occasionally to consider alternatives the computer might have mis-assessed. Humans are much weaker than computers now in general, but they operate differently, so you develop a feeling for where the computer's evaluation function (who has the better position, by how much) or horizon (how far ahead it looks) might not

capture something a Grandmaster can. Periodically you add a little textual comment for the next person who may build on your work and then email the analysis to the group.

We did debate contentious ideas and assessments of particular positions over the table, but mostly this was a prelude to stresstesting ideas in more depth with the computer. We would go back and try a range of plausible ideas and watch to see if the evaluation changed; a signal to look further for hidden details. At one point, feeling frustrated with my inability to make a dent on a particularly solid line, I got up to consider an idea on the actual chess set at the far end of the room under the main

window. I remember Peter smiling at me sympathetically but also incredulously, as if to say: 'If only it were that easy.'

Preparing with a world champion for a World Championship match was precious to me not because it was extraordinary but because it was mundane. I saw the grind behind the glory.

I witnessed the monotonous practice that precedes the magical performance. I was there when the groceries were bought and the dishes were washed. There was no heightened drama, just slow-burning determination, gentle discipline and professional friendship. The experience was precious in the way that

CHESS HAD ALWAYS BEEN A GUIDING FORCE IN HERBERT'S LIFE

BEREND VONK

AS A LOVER OF THE ITALIAN OPENING, IT FELT SO NATURAL TO MARRY MARIA going on a pilgrimage or running a marathon can be precious. It was a short pause in everyday existence, and a memorable plunge into another stream of life.

As for my contribution, I'm fairly sure I did not do any harm, and may even have helped a little. Vishy won the match decisively, not least because

It felt like work and it felt like the future, but not, I hoped, my work, or my future.

To give an illustration of how far the experience deviated from my expectations, I was in two minds about whether even to bring my computer to the training (a basic Sony Vaio laptop I had used for

considered pretty slow). Your cores are about your processing power, and speed matters because it saves a lot of analytical time. The faster the engine the quicker it can search ahead and determine which lines are good and bad before you get there manually. That filter helpfully narrows your own search process down to only those lines that are worth pursuing, and before you know it you can tell which opening lines are critical and ripe for analysis, and which are in some sense solved. That's important for the team because you can all trust each other to be looking at lines that matter; you know that if you're asked a question about a position it won't be a waste of time. Tactical details that arise almost by force several moves downstream are often hard to see coming for a human, but they are spotted almost instantly by the computer, changing the evaluation of that line before you need to explore it. It was only because I was literally up to speed with the others that I could enjoy several productive days at the camp.

When Vishy saw it on my screen he paused ruefully and said: 'Oh, Jon has only one core.' Kasim and Peter looked at each other, a little troubled.

the team as a whole (which included some other Grandmasters from India and Poland) succeeded over several months in developing a completely new repertoire for Vishy as White, based on a different first move – 1.d4 rather than 1.e4; the queen's pawn two squares forward rather than the king's pawn. That small difference entirely changes the nature of the game, creating different pawn structures calling for different strategies, and circumventing much of the opponent's preparation. An analogy would be a tennis player going into training for several months and emerging capable of serving well with either hand; a capability he only reveals in the final match against an unsuspecting opponent.

We succeeded in keeping that crucial first-move surprise a secret on the basis of personal trust, without any heavy-handed non-disclosure agreements, which is impressive given the high stakes. It was also clear to me that Vishy is impressively organised, and manages to generate an arsenal of chess information that is codified, relevant and valuable. So I was transfixed and impressed, and intrigued by the whole process. But at a professional level I was more alienated than inspired. This screen and data-intensive process was not chess as I have come to know and love it.

years). Very soon after arrival, before a pawn had been pushed, Vishy asked me: 'How many cores do you have, Jon?' (I prefer being called Jonathan, but had never told him this.)

'Oh, I'm not sure,' I said, which was clearly not a reassuring answer. Vishy talked me through finding the relevant details on my computer. When he saw it on my screen he paused ruefully and said: 'Oh, Jon has only one core.' Kasim and Peter looked at each other, a little troubled. I had no idea what was going on, but it was as if I had arrived at the border to a new country, only to learn that my passport was not valid.

Vishy looked mildly ruffled but said it did not matter, because it was possible to connect to online analysis engines – a mysterious notion at the time because I had never done that before, but it was a source of hope too. Alas, I then had painfully mundane problems relating to getting the wi-fi to work, and realised I was slowing the team down. I maintained a professional face, but inwardly I was approaching one of those childlike moments of absolute humiliation.

Mercifully, everything was soon sorted, and it was like finding water in the desert. For the first time I started looking at positions with a four-core analysis engine (which, at the time of writing a decade later, would be

But I will never forget that feeling of being an analogue creature, floundering in a digital world. ∎

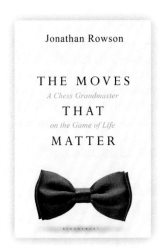

The Moves that Matter: A Chess Grandmaster on the Game of Life by Jonathan Rowson, is out now, published by Bloomsbury Publishing. Hardcover, 352 pages.

Creative Dare-devil

Daniil Dubov annotates brilliant win

Not only Magnus Carlsen says that he feels inspired by Daniil Dubov; more and more fans closely follow his adventurous games. The Russian GM looks at his best win from the European Team Championship in Batumi, where Russia took gold. Dubov contributed 5½ points from 7 games, with a 2805 performance.

NOTES BY
Daniil Dubov

Daniil Dubov
Rasmus Svane
Batumi 2019
Queen's Gambit Declined,
Blackburne Variation

This game was played in Round 7. We were playing a very solid German team and I had White against Rasmus Svane. Considering the fact that I didn't really feel well, the plan was to play it slow and safe. But this plan never works.
1.c4 e6 2.♘c3 d5 3.d4

I was kinda happy here. It was unlikely that he would play 3...♘f6 4.cxd5 ♘xd5, since he rarely plays this. And I am comfortably better after 3...♗e7 4.cxd5 exd5 5.♗f4. Things were going my way!
3...♘f6 Not really. **4.♘f3**
4.cxd5 ♘xd5, with numerous forced lines, wasn't what I wanted to play.
4...♗e7 Not even 4...dxc4, which he plays sometimes. Tough luck.
5.♗f4 0-0 6.e3 b6!? And now this. I had an idea about what I could play

After less than an hour I felt as if I was trying to save the match. Not an ideal scenario, but at least I like it when the math says I have to take risks.

after 6...c5 or 6...♘bd7, but this solid line was way too uninspiring.
7.♕c2!?

Obviously, the whole concept with castling queenside was over-the-board inspiration. It was actually a bit easier to do it when looking at the other boards, because the opening phase had finished in favour of the opposite team. Nikita Vitiugov, with Black on Board 1, was thinking in what looked like quite a dangerous position, whereas his opponent Nisipeanu was obviously still in book. Kirill Alekseenko was

Daniil Dubov lost in thought during his game against Rasmus Svane,
moments before he will play his knight to g5. 'That was my main point.'

9...♘c6!? This doesn't feel natural to me. I was much more worried about the set-up with ...♘bd7, as he would have ...♘dxf6 after ♗e5 or ♘ce4. Still, it seems like a complete mess, and in my analysis I failed to prove that Black was better:
9...♘bd7!? 10.h4, and now:

ANALYSIS DIAGRAM

– 10...b5 11.♘ce4 ♘xe4 12.♕xe4 ♘f6 13.♕c2 b4 14.♗xc4 ♗xc4 15.♕xc4, and after the fireworks it seems to be just equal.

– 10...h6?! 11.e4! hxg5 12.hxg5 ♘h7 13.e5 g6 14.♗e3.

– 10...♗d6 11.♗e5 h6 12.f4!

ANALYSIS DIAGRAM

and Black is in danger, which would only grow if we went more deeply. We could spend a few pages analysing the lines, so I'll just show one of them: 12...b5 13.♘ce4 ♘xe4 14.♕xe4 f5 15.♕c6 hxg5 16.hxg5 ♕c8 17.♕f3 ♗xe5 18.dxe5 ♔f7 19.g6+ ♔e7 20.e4! fxe4 21.♕g4, with a White advantage. These were the moves from Black's first lines, so even the engine fails to give the answer as to why Black should be better.

Instead, 9...g6 is right up White's

down 30 minutes against Fridman's 1:33 or so in a Petroff as White, and Black looked fine. Georg Meier had exchanged all the pieces and had offered a draw to Maxim Matlakov. So, basically, after less than an hour of play I felt as if I was trying to save the match. Not an ideal scenario, but at least I like situations when the math says I have to take risks.

7...♗a6 8.0-0-0

Now White is all-in. I was actually

quite pessimistic about the objective evaluation of this position, feeling that I was much worse. This doesn't seem to be correct, Black is only slightly, if at all, better.

8...dxc4! 8...♗xc4?! 9.♗xc4 dxc4 10.♕e2 is obviously less ambitious.

9.♘g5!?

That was my main point. I'll always face ...h6 with h4, following it up with ♗e5, f4 and so on. I was probably worse, but at least I felt that it wouldn't be comfortable for him.

alley: 10.h4 ♘d5 11.♘xh7 ♘xf4 12.exf4 ♔xh7 13.d5 e5 14.h5 ♔g7 15.fxe5 ♘d7 16.f4, and only White can be better.

10.a3 g6 11.h4

11...♗d6? I had expected 11...♘d5! 12.♘xd5 exd5 13.♗e2 (13.g4!?).

ANALYSIS DIAGRAM

Again, I was quite pessimistic about the objective evaluation, but at least I could take on h7 or do some other aggressive stuff, so there would be no joy for him. But, in fact, White is not even worse: 13...♗c8! (13...b5? is met by 14.♘xh7) 14.g4 h6!? 15.♘xf7 ♔xf7 16.h5 ♖g8 17.♗xh6 ♗f8 18.hxg6+ ♖xg6 19.♗f4, and White attacks, is one of the lines.

12.g3!

A very stylish move that was partly inspired by my friend Alexander Riazantsev, who likes to play ...♗f5, followed by ...e6, ...g6 and ...h5, in the Caro-Kann.

Black's attack is too slow, so he is basically lost. It's not that often that you see Black being lost after one mistake in the QGD! Well, it was only beginning...

12...♕e7

After 12...♗xf4 13.gxf4 ♗b7 14.h5 ♘b4 15.axb4 ♗xh1 16.hxg6 hxg6 17.f3 (or even 17.♘xe6!?) Black might as well resign.

13.h5 e5

14.hxg6

A decent move, but there was a much easier way.

It's sad that I completely forgot about 14.♘xh7!?, finishing the game immediately: 14...exf4 15.hxg6 fxg6 16.♗g2, and White wins, or 14...♘xh7 15.hxg6 exf4 16.g7 f5 17.gxf8♕+ ♖xf8 18.gxf4, and wins.

14...hxg6 15.♗g2 exf4

16.♗xc6?

Well, my problem was that I didn't know how much better I was. Taking

on c6, followed by ♘d5 or ♕a4, looked so tempting, as he didn't even have extra material. Not that Black isn't lost anymore, but it's way less obvious now.

After 16.gxf4!, which I had been considering for 10 minutes, it would have been over: 16...♕d7 17.♘d5 ♔g7 18.♘xf6 ♔xf6

ANALYSIS DIAGRAM

and now White has a choice:
– 19.♘h7+ ♔e7 (19...♔g7 20.f5) 20.♕e4+, and wins.
– Or 19.♖h7, also winning.

The reason I didn't play it was mostly that I thought it was just too much, and it looked more like showing off to me compared to the solid 16.♗xc6. And you know what? I actually don't really regret it.

16...fxg3!

17.♔b1!

This is what I'm mostly proud of in this game, since it's never easy to push yourself and play a good move after a terrible mistake. Indeed, I realized that it's not easy anymore, since there's no mate with ♘d5, so the game starts again. I decided to prepare fxg3 or f4.

Petersburg, December 2018. A friendly joke between World Blitz Champion Magnus Carlsen and World Rapid Champion Daniil Dubov.

31.♕h8+ ♖g8 32.♕h6+ ♔e8 33.♕h5+ ♔d7 34.♕h3+, with a perpetual and a draw.
23.♕xg6+

23...♔f8 And not 23...♖g7? 24.♗xd5+ ♔f8 25.♘h7+ ♖xh7 26.♕g8 mate. **24.♕h6+ ♖g7 25.♗xd5**

25...♔e8? In fact, he had to play 25...♗f5+! 26.e4 ♔e8!, which would have led to a draw: 27.♗c6+ (I'd probably try 27.exf5, even though this should also be a draw after 27...♕xe1+ 28.♔a2 ♖xg5 29.♗c6+ ♖d7 30.fxg5 ♗f8 31.♕e6+ ♕xe6 32.fxe6) 27...♗d7 28.♕h5+ ♔f8 29.♕h6 ♗xc6 30.♕h8+ ♖g8 31.♕h6+ ♔e8 32.♕h5+ ♔d7 33.♕h3+, with another perpetual.
26.♕h5+ ♔d7 27.♕h3+ ♔e8 28.♕h5+ ♔d7
It was quite important that I was down to seven minutes here, so repeating the moves once wasn't a bad idea. I wasn't

17...♖ad8 18.f4?
Unfortunately, my emotional comeback didn't last long. I couldn't stop trying to make the ideas with mating on the h-file work, so I just went for the most straightforward line.
The thing is that I should have readjusted, and realized that it was time to push my pawns instead of trying to mate immediately: 18.fxg3! ♔g7 (18...♗xg3 19.♘ge4 ♘xe4 20.♗xe4 ♔g7 21.♖dg1, winning) 19.e4 ♖h8 (19...♗c8 20.♕c1) 20.♖xh8 ♖xh8 21.♖f1, and wins.
So, yeah, objectively speaking, I didn't, in fact, miss a win with 16.♗xc6, but it just became much trickier, as you can see.
18...♗c8!

Now Black is fine again, but I finally got a few thoughts about what I could do next.
19.♖de1 ♔g7 20.♘d5! ♘xd5 21.♖h7+ ♔g8 22.♖xf7!

That was my idea.
22...♖xf7 22...♘c3+!? was also fine, but it doesn't change much: 23.bxc3 ♖xf7 24.♕xg6+ ♔f8 25.♕h6+ ♖g7 26.♗d5 ♗f5+! 27.e4 ♔e8 28.♗c6+ ♗d7 29.♕h5+ ♔f8 30.♕h6 ♗xc6

Unfortunately, my emotional comeback didn't last long. I couldn't stop trying to make the ideas with mating on the h-file work.

sure about what would happen after 29.♗e6+, but I was certainly tempted to play it. After seeing that Nikita was still lost I didn't have a choice, which always feels good.

29.♗e6+! ♔c6!?

Of course he had to try this in time-trouble.

I think it was obvious to both of us that White was much better after 29...♕xe6! 30.♘xe6 ♔xe6 31.f5+ ♔e7 32.e4!, etc. Maybe Black can hold this, but I failed to find a clear way.

30.♕f3+ ♔b5 31.♗xc4+

31...♔a5

It's quite strange that originally I was a bit more worried about 31...♔xc4 32.♕c6+ ♗c5 33.♖c1+ ♔d3

ANALYSIS DIAGRAM

It's my favourite kind of game: two strong players have no idea of what's going on and neither do the stupid chessbomb viewers and a very big number of so-called experts.

and it took me a couple of minutes to find 34.♖c3+ ♔e2 35.♕g2+ ♔e1 36.♖c1, mate.

Somehow I was much more optimistic about 31...♔a5, as I was sure that it should be winning for me, but at this point I didn't see clearly how.

32.♕d5+

32...♗c5 Black will be mated after 32...c5: 33.b4+ ♔a4 34.♗b3+ ♔b5 (34...♔xa3 35.♗c2) 35.a4+ ♔xb4 36.♕c4+ ♔a3 37.♗c2 ♗e6 38.♕c3+ ♗b3 39.♕xb3, mate. **33.b4+ ♔a4**

34.♕g2! I like this study-like idea. First I provoke ...♗xb4 to take away that square from the king.

34...♗xb4 35.♕c6+ ♔xa3

36.♗b3! Playing this move with only 10 seconds on the clock is quite memorable, of course. It's also funny that it's the only move, not only to win the game, but even not to lose it!

36...♗d7 If 36...♔xb3 then 37.♕c2+ and mate. **37.♕c1+ ♔xb3 38.♕c2+ ♔a3 39.♕a2** Mate.

It was so nice of him to allow this checkmate, which I'm grateful for.

Less than a minute after finishing the game I told our captain that it had taken too much from me and that I desperately needed to have a rest the next day.

All in all, it's my favourite kind of game: two strong players have no idea of what's going on and neither do the stupid chessbomb viewers and a very big number of so-called experts, who prefer posting and tweeting about your mistakes instead of checking things carefully.

I also want to thank the whole team and our coaches, who did an enormous job. Somehow all the world thinks that Russia should win all the time and that it normally comes easy. But this time we didn't have our strongest line-up; we failed to win in the first round and had to face a lot of tricky circumstances. Yet, we still managed to win. ■

1. Spyropoulos-David
Anogia 2019

White finds the way to crash through: **45.♕xh6!** Black resigned in view of 45...gxh6 (if 45...♗xd6 46.♖xg7, mating) 46.♖xg8+ ♖xg8 47.♘xf7 mate.

2. David-Katopodis
Anogia 2019

47.♖d5! The king is the real target: 47...exd5 48.♕xd5+ ♔xf6 (48...♔e8 49.♕e6+) 49.♕e5+ ♔f7 50.♗d5 mate. Black resigned.

3. Xiong-Belous
Irving 2019

43.♖c8! White creates the threat of ♖c5 mate. **43...♖xe1 44.♖a4!** Now mate is inevitable. Black resigned.

4. Bogosavljevic-Damjanovic
Serbia 2019

39.♕xc5! Gaining access to the e4-square for the bishop. **39...♕xc5 40.♗e4+ ♔h5 41.♔h3!** With g2-g4 mate on the next move. Black resigned.

5. Vestby-Ellingsen-Bogner
Hell 2019

29...♖xd3! White resigned since after 30.cxd3 ♖c8 he will have to give up a whole rook (31.♖e1 or 31.♖ae6) to protect the back rank.

6. Koneru-Kashlinskaya
Skolkovo 2019

18.♘eg5! ♗xf3 If 18...hxg5 19.♘xg5 g6, 20.♘xf7! or any capture on e6 is devastating. **19.♕h7+ ♔f8 20.♖xe6!** 20...fxe6 21.♘xe6+ regains material and White's attack is in full swing. Black resigned.

7. Skembris-Nagy
Spilimbergo 2019

51...♘d2+ 52.♔g2 52.♔g1 ♘f3+! 53.♗xf3 ♖e1 mate; 52.♔f2 ♘c4+ 53.♔f1 (53.♔f3 ♖e3 mate) 53...♘e3+ 54.♔g1 ♘xd5. **52...♖e2+ 53.♔h3** Has the king reached safety? **53...♖h2+! 54.♔xh2 ♘f3+** With 55...♖h2 mate next. White resigned.

8. Charochkina-Kashlinskaya
Izhevsk 2019

37...♖xc1! 38.♖xc1 ♕xb2 The threat of ...♗e5 is hard to deal with. **39.♖c8+** 39.♖b1 ♕c3; 39.♖c2 ♕a1. **39...♔g7 40.♗xe4** 40.♖e8 ♕a1 41.h4 ♕g1+ 42.♔h3 ♕h1+ 43.♔h2 ♗xg2+ loses the queen. **40...♗e5** and Black soon won.

9. Cheparinov-Wang Hao
Changsha 2019

30.♖e6! ♗xe6 After 30...fxe6 31.dxe6 ♕e7 32.♖xd8 ♖xd8 33.♗xf6 ♕xf6 34.e7+ ♔g7 White had to have seen 35.♘d5! ♖xd5 36.e8♘+!, winning. **31.dxe6 ♕e5 32.e7 ♖xd1 33.exf8♕+ ♔xf8 34.♕xd1** and Black resigned shortly after.

An Endgame idea versus the Caro-Kann

Jeroen Bosch

3.d3!?

Rather than protecting e4 with the queen's knight, White uses his d-pawn for that purpose, which immediately allows Black to trade queens.

The Caro-Kann is popular again these days, which is partly because 1.e4 c6 2.d4 d5 3.♘c3 dxe4 4.♘xe4 ♘f6 5.♘xf6+ exf6!? isn't all that easy to meet.

White players, meanwhile, have been seeking alternative ways to meet the Caro-Kann. The popularity of the London led to renewed interest in the Exchange Variation. Indeed, 1.d4 d5 2.♗f4 c5 3.e3 cxd4 4.exd4 is a Caro-Kann Exchange!

Other players, most notably Vachier-Lagrave, have been playing the Two Knights Variation successfully: 1.e4 c6 2.♘f3 d5 3.♘c3.

But this is too theoretical for us, so we will concentrate on the odd 1.e4 c6 2.♘f3 d5 3.d3!?, which has been played by Anish Giri, Levon Aronian, Vassily Ivanchuk and Jorden van Foreest.

1.e4 c6 2.♘f3 d5 3.d3

Rather than protecting e4 with the queen's knight, White uses his d-pawn for that purpose, which immediately allows Black to trade queens – which is the principled response. Note that against other moves White is certainly not obliged to transpose to some kind of King's Indian Reversed. Indeed, after 2.d3 d5 3.♘d2 (3.♘f3 is our SOS line again!) Black has the satisfactory 3...e5, which is not an option now.

3...dxe4

Despite a neat double attack, Black should not play 3...e5?! 4.♘xe5 dxe4 5.♘c3! (5.dxe4?? ♕a5+).

There are two serious alternatives to taking on e4.

■ The first is 3...♗g4 4.h3 ♗h5 (the fact that White hasn't developed his queen's knight yet after 4...♗xf3 5.♕xf3 should favour him compared to the similar line in the Two Knights Variation: 5...e6 6.g3 ♘d7 7.♗g2 ♘gf6 8.♕e2 ♕c7 9.♘d2 0-0-0 10.0-0 h5 11.♘f3 was very pleasant for White in Rakotomaharo-E.Atalik, Douglas 2019).

White will now start to harass Black's bishop with a combination of g4 and h4. Let's look at two games:

– 5.♕e2 e6 6.g4 ♗g6 7.h4 h6 (7...h5 8.♘e5 ♗h7 9.g5 dxe4 threatens ...♕a5+, but 10.♘c3 ♕c7 – 10...exd3 11.♕xh5 ♕c7 12.♘xd3± – 11.♗f4 ♗d6 12.♘xf7!? – 12.d4 – 12...♔xf7 13.♕xh5+ is dangerous for Black) 8.♘bd2 (8.h5 ♗h7 9.g5 is unclear) 8...♘d7 9.♗g2 (9.h5!?) 9...♗e7 (9...h5!) 10.h5 ♗h7 11.♘b3 dxe4 12.dxe4

♘gf6 13.g5 hxg5 14.♘xg5 ♗g8 was Santos Ruiz-Ivanchuk, Forni di Sopra 2019, and here 15.f4 or 15.♗d2 leads to interesting positions in which the bishop on g8 looks odd.

– 5.♘c3 e6 6.g4 ♗g6 7.♕e2 (also interesting is the immediate 7.h4!? dxe4 (7...h5?! 8.♘e5 ♗h7 9.g5 favours White) 8.h5 ♗xh5 9.♘e5! ♗g6 10.♘xg6 fxg6) 7...d4 8.♘b1 c5 (8... h5!?) 9.h4 h5 10.♘e5 ♗h7 11.g5 ♕c7

12.♘c4 (12.♕f3!? loses no time with the knight in the centre: 12...♗d6 13.♘c4 ♗g6 14.♘ba3 a6 15.♘xd6+ ♕xd6 16.♘c4, with a superior position; also good is 12...♘c6 13.♘xc6 ♕xc6 14.♕xh5, and after 12...♕xe5?? 13.♗f4 White wins the queen) 12...♗g6?! 13.a4, and White was doing great in Giri-Nepomniachtchi, Amsterdam 2019.

■ Black has also tried 3...g6 4.e5!? (4.♘bd2 ♗g7 transposes to a King's Indian Attack).

And now 4...♗g7 5.d4 ♗g4 6.♘bd2 f6 7.h3 ♗xf3 8.♘xf3 favoured White in Delorme-Matnadze, Linares 2019. More to the point are 4...c5 and 4...♗g4:

– 4...c5 5.c3 ♘c6 6.d4 ♗g4

7.dxc5 (7.♘bd2!? cxd4 8.cxd4 f6?! – 8...♕a5! 9.♕b3 ♕b4 10.♗b5 is about equal – 9.♗b5 fxe5 10.dxe5 ♗g7 11.♕a4 ♕b6?? 12.♗xc6+ Leko-Georgiadis, Biel 2019; 7.♗b5 is the main move – this position usually arises after 1.e4 c5 2.♘f3 g6 3.c3 d5 4.e5 ♘c6 5.d4 ♗g4 6.♗b5, when both sides haven't lost a move: d3-d4 and ...c6-c5 occur in our Caro-Kann) 7...♗xf3 8.♕xf3 ♘xe5?! (8...♗g7! 9.♗b5 ♗xe5) 9.♗b5+ ♘c6 10.c4 ♘f6 11.♘c3 (11.0-0) 11...dxc4? (11... d4 12.♗xc6+ bxc6 13.♕xc6+ ♘d7 14.♘d5±) 12.♗xc6+ bxc6 13.♕xc6+ ♘d7 14.♗e3 ♗g7, J.van Foreest-Tari, chess.com 2019, and now 15.0-0-0 is the cleanest win.

– 4...♗g4 5.♘bd2 (5.d4 c5 6.♗b5+ ♘c6 7.c3 transposes to the Sicilian that we mentioned above after 4...c5, but White also has 7.dxc5) 5...c5 6.h3 ♗f5 7.d4 cxd4 8.♘xd4 ♘c6 9.♗b5 ♗d7. Black has lost too many tempi playing his bishop back and forth.

Now, rather than 10.e6 fxe6 11.♗xc6 bxc6 12.♘2b3 ♗g7 13.0-0 e5∓, J.van Foreest-Tari, chess.com 2019, White should have played 10.♗xc6 bxc6 11.0-0 ♗g7 12.♘2f3±.

4.dxe4 ♕xd1+ 5.♔xd1

And so after five moves a 'simple' queenless middlegame has arisen. It's a draw, of course, but so is the starting position. White has a slight edge in development. Clearly, Ulf Andersson in his heyday (think of the well-known positional masterpiece Andersson-Tempone, Buenos Aires 1979) would have enjoyed playing on the white side – and, judging by recent games, so do Levon Aronian and Anish Giri.

5...♘f6

■ The other main try is 5...♗g4, when White has several ways to respond. On the whole, there is no need to memorize moves in this line. Just play through the game fragments to get a feel for these positions.

– 6.♘bd2 ♘d7 7.♗e2 e5 8.h3 ♗h5 9.♘e1 ♗xe2+ (9...♗g6) 10.♔xe2 ♘c5 11.f3 ♘e6 12.c3 (12.♘d3) 12...♘f4+ 13.♔f1?! (13.♔d1) 13...0-0-0 (13...♘h5! 14.♖h2 ♗c5! threatens mate as well as trapping the silly rook on h2: 15.g4 ♘g3+ 16.♔g2 ♘e2, and the engine insists on zeros but a human would prefer Black) 14.♘b3 ♘e6 15.♗e3 ♔b8 16.♔e2 ♘f6 17.♘d3 ♗d6 18.♖hd1 ♗c7 19.a4 a5 20.♘d2 ♘d7 21.♘c4 g6 22.b4!, with a strong attack on the queenside in J.van Foreest-Tari, chess.com 2019.

– 6.♗e3 ♘d7 (6...♗xf3+ 7.gxf3 ♘d7 8.♘d2 e6 9.♘c4 – it makes sense to include 9.♖g1!? – 9...♗c5 10.♗d3 ♗xe3 11.fxe3 ♔e7 12.f4 ♘gf6 13.♔e2 ♘c5 14.♔f3, Timofeev-Faizrakhmanov, Kazan 2019, and now Black had the strong positional pawn sacrifice 14...g5!: 15.fxg5 ♘fd7 16.b4 b5 17.♘a5 ♘e5+) 7.♘bd2 e5 8.♗c4 ♗c5 9.♔e2 ♗xe3 10.♔xe3 ♘gf6 11.h3 ♗xf3 12.♘xf3 ♔e7 13.♖hd1 ♘b6?!. This appears to win a tempo for re-grouping the pieces (...♘f6-d7 and ...f7-f6 is the idea), it fails to a fine exchange sacrifice: 14.♘xe5! ♘fd7 15.♖xd7+! (15.♘xd7 ♘xc4+ 16.♔f4 ♘xb2) 15...♘xd7 16.♘xf7 ♖hf8 17.♘g5 b5 18.♗b3 a5 19.a3, and with two central pawns for the exchange White was better in Ivanchuk-Vidit, Doha 2016. – 6.♗e2 ♘d7 7.♘d4, forcing the trade of the light-squared bishops, but they will be exchanged after most normal moves: 7...♗xe2+ 8.♔xe2 e5 9.♘b3 a5 10.a4 ♘c5 11.♘1d2 ♘f6 12.f3 ♘fd7 13.♘xc5 ♗xc5 14.♘c4 ♔e7.

Of the many innocuous-looking positions in this article, this one is as good as any to briefly reflect upon. Material is equal, with a symmetrical pawn structure. The queens and two sets of minor pieces have already come off, and we may wonder when the rest will be traded down to a boring draw. And yet, White already has a substantial advantage! White's bishop is stronger than its counterpart, his knight is slightly more active (it attacks while Black's knight is defending), and most important of all: pawn a5 is a weakness. See how quickly Van Foreest achieves a completely winning position: 15.♗d2! b6 (protecting a5 but Black's pawn chain

will remain weak: if only the pawn on c6 were on c7) 16.♖hd1 ♔e6? (16...f6) 17.♗e3! (paradoxical but strong – the 'bad' bishop on c5 is protecting pawn b6 and square d6. So White should trade off the defender!) 17...♖hd8 (or 17...♗xe3 18.♔xe3, and Black has no satisfactory defence to the threats of 19.♖xd7 and 19.♖d6+) 18.♗xc5 ♘xc5 19.♖xd8 ♖xd8 20.♘xb6, and White was winning in J.van Foreest-Tari, chess.com 2019.

■ Navara has twice gone for 5...f6!?.

– Against Ivanchuk, Navara obtained equal chances after 6.♗e3 e5 7.♘bd2 ♗g4 (7...♘d7) 8.h3 ♗xf3+ (after 8...♗h5 9.g4 both 9...♗f7 10.♗c4 and 9...♗g6 10.h4 h5 11.g5 favour White) 9.♘xf3 ♘d7 10.♗c4 ♗c5 11.♔e2 ♗xe3 12.♔xe3 ♘e7 13.c3 0-0-0 14.h4 ♔c7, Ivanchuk-Navara, Huaian rapid 2016.
– In a recent game from the European Team Championship in Batumi, Aronian went for 6.♘e1!? e5 7.♗c4 ♘d7 8.f3 ♘c5 9.♗e3. Black has set up a normal structure with ...f6 and ...e5. Yet, White holds a slight edge, which in the game looked even larger after 9...♗e6 10.♘d2 ♗xc4 11.♘xc4 0-0-0+ 12.♔e2 ♔b8 13.♘d3 ♘xd3 14.♖ad1!? (14.cxd3) 14...♘e7 15.cxd3 ♘g6 16.g3 ♗d6 17.♘xd6! ♖xd6 18.h4 h5 19.f4

and White held on to the initiative in this endgame (f4-f5 and g4 is coming). Aronian-Navara, Batumi 2019.

■ Another model game from White's point of view went 5...♘d7 6.♘fd2 e5 7.f3 ♗d6 8.a4 ♘gf6 9.c3 0-0 10.♔c2 ♗c7 11.♘b3 ♖d8 12.♘a3 b6?! (this weakening of the structure is best avoided) 13.♗e3 ♘f8 14.♗e2 ♘e6 15.♖hd1.

White is often happy to trade one set of rooks, but not both – he needs one rook for play on the queenside or kingside. 15...♖xd1 16.♖xd1 ♔f8 17.♘c1 ♔e7 18.♘d3 ♘d7 19.♘b4 (White is creating threats) 19...♘b8 (19...♗b7 20.♗a6! and the weakness of pawn c6 will count for something) 20.♘c4, and Black had an unpleasant position and lost in Theodorou-Shimanov, chess.com 2019.

6.♘fd2!?

Giri's choice (White goes for the familiar set-up with f3), but certainly not the only move.
Black merely gets squares for his pieces after 6.e5?! ♘d5, and also playable is 6...♘g4 7.♘e1 ♘d7, when 8.e6! fxe6 is about equal.
Natural is 6.♘bd2 g6!? (here 6...♗g4 7.♗e2 ♘bd7 8.♘e1 ♗xe2+ 9.♔xe2 ♘c5 10.f3 ♘fd7 11.♘c4 g6 was Yankelevich-Teja, Vienna 2019, and now 12.♗e3 ♗g7 13.♘d3 would have been a bit better for White) 7.c3 ♗g7 8.♘e1 ♗g4 9.♘d3 ♘d7 10.♘c4 0-0 (White is still a bit better after 10...♘de5 11.♘cxe5 ♘xe5 12.♔c2) 11.f3 ♘ge5 12.♘dxe5 ♘xe5 13.♗e3 ♗e6 14.♘xe5 ♗xe5 15.♔c2 a5 16.a4 f5, J.van Foreest-Marti-

rosyan, chess.com 2019, and now 17.exf5 ♗xf5+ 18.♗d3 is still a little something.

6...♘g4

Black likewise manoeuvres his king's knight around. Practice has also seen:
■ 6...g6 7.f3 ♗g7 8.a4 0-0 9.c3 ♘bd7 10.♘b3 ♘e5 11.♗e3 ♘e8 12.♘1d2 (White has played his by now familiar set-up. Black is seeking counterplay) 12...f5!? 13.exf5 gxf5 (Black can aim for piece activity with 13...♗xf5, but the pawn structure is more important here after, say, 14.♘d4 ♗d7 15.♘c4) 14.f4 ♘g4 15.♗g1 ♘d6 16.♔c2 and a draw was agreed in Santos Ruiz-Dreev, Forni di Sopra 2019. Black still has to justify the weakening of his structure, though.
■ Black had not fully solved his problems after 6...♘bd7 7.f3 g6 8.♘b3 h5 9.♗e3 ♘h6 10.♗f2 ♘b6 11.c3 ♗e6 12.♘c5 0-0-0+ 13.♔c2 ♗c4 14.b3 ♗xf1 15.♖xf1 in Todorov-Villegas, Brest 2018.

7.♔e1 e5 8.♘c4 After 8.♘b3 Black should consider 8...a5 9.a4 ♗e6 10.♘1d2 (or 10.f3 ♗xb3! 11.cxb3 ♗b4+) 10...♘a6!?. Instead, after 8...♘d7 9.f3 ♘gf6 10.♗e3 ♗d6 11.♘1d2 ♘e7 12.a4 a5 13.♘c4 ♗c7, Piskur-Neuman, Aschach 2010, White has achieved his 'normal edge'.

8...b5 Black forces a knight swap, but it comes at a price. Pawn b5 is a clear target for White. Note that the active 8...♗c5?! is strongly met by 9.f3 ♘f2 10.b4!.

9.♘e3 Not 9.♘cd2? ♗c5. **9...♗c5 10.♘xg4 ♗xg4 11.a4! b4 12.a5** Very ambitious: White is 'isolating' Black's b-pawn. Conventional moves

are 12.♘d2, 12.f3, and 12.♗c4. In all cases White is more comfortable due to the weak squares within Black's queen-side formation.

12...♘d7 13.♗c4 ♔e7 14.♘d2 ♗d6 15.f3 ♗e6 16.♗xe6 ♔xe6 17.♘c4

Clearly White's opening strategy has been successful. Both his minor pieces are superior to their black counterparts, and he has an edge on the queenside.

17...♖ab8 18.♔e2 ♗c5 19.♖d1 f6 20.♗e3!?

Just as Van Foreest did in one of his games against Tari, Giri is exchanging Black's 'bad' bishop on purpose. The bishop is a defender of square d6 here. It was also sensible to continue with useful moves like 20.♗d2 or the space-gaining 20.h4.

20...♗xe3 21.♔xe3 ♔e7 22.♖d6! ♖hc8 23.♖ad1

So Giri has taken control of the only open file. Note how all his pieces are better placed than Black's.

23...♘c5 24.g3!

A new front is needed, this prepares f3-f4.

24...♖c7 25.f4 exf4+ 26.gxf4 ♖b5? **27.♖g1** Even stronger was 27.♖d8!, but then you need to calculate 27...♘b7

28.♖a8! (or 28.♖g8! ♔f7 29.♖b8, but not 28.♖b8? ♘xa5!, and Black wins) 28...♘xa5 29.♘d6!.

27...g6 28.f5! b3 29.c3 ♔f7? More tenacious was 29...♘d7. **30.e5! fxe5 31.fxg6+ ♔g7** Black loses the house after 31...hxg6 32.♖dxg6. **32.gxh7+ ♔xh7 33.♖dg6!**

Setting up a familiar mate with two rooks.

33...♖b8 34.♖6g5 ♔h8 35.♖xe5 ♘a4 36.♖a1! Winning the knight and the game. **36...♘xc3 37.bxc3 ♖h7 38.♔d4 ♖xh2 39.♖b1 ♖h3 40.♘d6 ♖d8 41.♖e8+** 1-0, Giri-Nepomniachtchi, Amsterdam 2019.

So, how should we evaluate this SOS? On the one hand, it's an extremely early opening surprise, which immediately leads the game away from long and forced variations. On the other hand, you might feel that the resulting positions (without queens) are 'boring' and ought to be close to equal. The fact that some of the best players have been willing to go for this queenless middlegame to play for a win should count for something. In the end, I suppose it comes down to taste. If your heroes in chess are Capablanca, Karpov, Kramnik (the player who became World Champion by trading off Kasparov's queen as quickly as possible) and the endgame-grinder Carlsen (there are several versions of this World Champion – he is also a dynamic attacking player when he wants to), then this is a line for you. If Kasparov and Tal are more to your taste, then 3.d3 is not for you, I am afraid. ■

Judit Polgar

Hand and Brain

It's an attractive form of chess that requires mutual understanding and a wish to work together. The stronger player on the team says whether 'a piece' or 'a pawn' has to be moved and the other player makes the move. At the Global Chess Festival in Budapest, the first official 'hand-and-brain' tournament was held. Chief organizer **JUDIT POLGAR** loved what she saw.

For many centuries, chess has basically remained an individual game, even though we also have team events like the Olympiads, which have taken place regularly ever since the early 20th century. This is a bit of a pity if we compare chess to, say, tennis and table tennis, where double matches, with real interaction between the team mates, are an important part of the competition system.

That's why I staged the first 'hand-and-brain' tournament during this year's Global Chess Festival. It was a special attraction for the online audience, for people who could not travel to Budapest to watch the multitude of activities at the Festival. I was animated by the thought that this entertaining system of play demands a close connection between the team mates, and requires mutual understanding and, if you wish, the ability to read the other's mind. In order to make the event even more 'colourful', I asked the Russian painter Mariya Yugina to make a piece of art illustrating the hand-and-brain concept, which was used as the tournament's

logo. Mariya has painted a whole series of chess paintings over the past several years and is a passionate player herself. The tournament's name, 'The Inspiration Cup', was suggested by one of the members of the Game Changers team, Natasha Regan.

According to the rules, the lower-rated player indicates a piece, for instance by saying 'knight' and his or her partner has to move a knight, but must decide him- or herself which one (if there is more than one available), and where it will go to. The rhythm of play was eight minutes per game with a two-second increment per move. When a team was left with less than a minute on the clock, one of the players could take over to complete the game without waiting for his or her partner's suggestions.

It was rewarding that all four invited teams accepted my idea with enthusiasm. We had three married couples and a team of co-authors, meaning that they all knew each other pretty well and could understand each other's thoughts. Each team had at least one grandmaster.

The semi-finals consisted of one game each, with a 'sudden-death' game to

follow in case of a draw, while the final was scheduled for two games and an Armageddon if necessary.

Before drawing conclusions about the hand-and brain system, I invite you to watch some of the most interesting moments of the tournament.

Sofia Polgar & Yona Kosashvili
Mariya Yugina & Mihail Marin
Global Chess 2019 (1)
French Defence, Exchange Variation
1.e4 e6 2.d4 d5 3.exd5 exd5
4.♘f3 ♘f6 5.♗g5 ♗e6 6.♗d3
♗e7 7.0-0 0-0 8.h3 c5 9.dxc5
♗xc5 10.c3 ♘c6 11.♘bd2 h6
12.♗h4 g5

13.♘b3

When Sofia said 'knight' she may have had in mind 13.♘xg5 hxg5 14.♗xg5, offering White good attacking possibilities. But since Black can resolve the pin with ...♗e7 at any time, the evaluation is not entirely clear.

13...♗d6

Mihail felt the danger and kept the bishop close to e7. If 13...♗b6? then Black will be in trouble after 14.♘xg5 hxg5 15.♗xg5.

14.♗g3 ♗xg3 15.fxg3 ♘e4 16.♕e1 f5 17.♘fd4 ♗d7 18.♖d1 ♕b6 19.g4 ♖ae8 20.gxf5 ♗xf5 21.♔h1?

Safer was 21.♗xe4 ♗xe4, when the strong e4-bishop compensates for the kingside weaknesses.

21...♘f2+!

Mariya thought for a long time, leaving her team with just one minute on the clock. She mainly considered 21...♕c7, which seems sound enough: 22.♘xf5 (after 22.♗xe4 ♗xe4 23.♖xf8+ ♖xf8, 24.♘e6? is a bad idea in view of 24...♕c8 25.♘xf8 ♕xh3 and mate) 22...♖xf5 23.♗xe4 ♖xf1+ 24.♕xf1 dxe4, with unclear play.

While trying to guess what his wife was thinking about (21...♗g6 looks natural and good), Mihail suddenly saw the small combination played in the game. And when the time dropped to under one minute, he took over to deliver.

22.♕xf2 ♗xd3 23.♖xd3 ♖xf2 24.♖xf2 ♖e1+ 25.♔h2

Black should win this position, but with such little time on clock he did not find a way to break White's fortress.

25...♕c7+ 26.g3 ♕e5 27.♘f3 ♕f5 28.♖dd2 ♖e3 29.♘bd4 ♕e4 30.♖de2 ♘xd4 31.♘xd4 ♖xe2 32.♖xe2 ♕b1 33.a3 ♕f1 34.g4 a6 35.♔g3 ♕f4+ 36.♔g2 ♕c1 37.♘f5 ♕d1 38.♖f2 ♔h7 39.♘d4 ♕b1 40.♘f5 ♕e4+ 41.♔g3 ♕e5+ 42.♔g2 ♕e4+ 43.♔g3 ♕e5+ Draw.

The Dracarys team (my sister Sofia and her husband Yona Kosashvili)

The hand-and-brain 'logo' at the Global Chess Festival was painted by Mariya Yugina.

won a dramatic Armageddon game to qualify for the final. The other finalists were the Game Changers team, which had defeated Olala Samurais (Tatyana Plachkinova and Arthur Kogan). The first game of the final seemed to be a long positional squeeze for Dracarys, until an interesting tactical moment arose.

**Sofia Polgar & Yona Kosashvili
Natasha Regan & Matthew Sadler**
Global Chess Festival 2019 (4)
Alekhine Defence, Larsen Variation

1.e4 ♘f6 2.e5 ♘d5 3.d4 d6 4.♘f3 dxe5 5.♘xe5 c6 6.♗c4 ♗f5 7.♕f3 e6

8.♗d3

The other way to weaken Black's structure was 8.♘xf7 ♔xf7 9.g4.

8...♕f6 9.♗xf5 exf5 10.0-0 ♗d6 11.c4 ♘e7 12.♖e1 0-0 13.♘c3 ♘g6 14.♕e2 ♖d8 15.f4 h6 16.♗e3 ♘d7 17.♖ad1 ♖ac8

We had three married couples and a team of co-authors, meaning that they all knew each other pretty well.

18.♕f3 ♘df8 19.♗f2 a6 20.g3 ♘e6

Black's slow manoeuvring has allowed White to consolidate their space advantage.

21.d5?

The trickiest situation in a hand-and-brain game arises when a pawn is indicated, since there are quite a few possibilities. The game continuation is thematic, but premature for tactical reasons. Instead, 21.h4! was the most effective pawn move, with White not only threatening to increase their space advantage with h4-h5, but also to take control of g5 in order to make d4-d5 a crushing threat.

21...♘g5?

'Knight' was the natural reaction from Natasha, but Matthew already felt that there were some tactics in the air. Instead of considering withdrawing the attacked knight, he investigated both the game continuation and 21...♘xe5! 22.fxe5 ♘g5, winning the e5-pawn, for instance 23.♕e2 ♗xe5, and the bishop is taboo in view of the fork on f3. He preferred the other knight move,

because he thought that in this latter position it would be much better to have a knight instead of a bishop on e5. But he had overlooked a cunning combination.

22.fxg5 ♘xe5

23.♖xe5! One of those situations in which 'rook' can mean only one thing. **23...♕xe5 24.♖e1** Suddenly the queen is trapped. The game soon entered the one-on-one phase, but despite his inventive rook manoeuvring Matthew could not save the day. **24...♕xe1+ 25.♗xe1 hxg5 26.♕xf5** And White won (1-0, 61).

In the second game, Caïssa seemed to smile on Dracarys again for a long time.

Natasha Regan & Matthew Sadler
Sofia Polgar & Yona Kosashvili
Global Chess Festival 2019 (5)
Italian Game, Giuoco Piano

1.e4 e5 2.♘f3 ♘c6 3.♗c4 ♗c5 4.c3 ♘f6 5.d3 0-0 6.♗g5 h6 7.♗h4 ♗e7 8.♗b3 d6 9.♘bd2 ♗e6 10.0-0 a6 11.d4 exd4 12.cxd4 ♗g4 13.d5 ♘e5

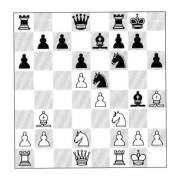

14.♖e1?

Lawrence Trent adds further entertainment after the final between Game Changers (Natasha Regan and Matthew Sadler) and Dracarys (Sofia Polgar and Yona Kosashvili).

One way or another, 'rook' loses a pawn. 14.♗g3 was better, even though Black has good play.

14...♘xd5! 15.♗xd5 ♗xh4 16.♗xb7

This only makes things worse, since the rook will exert lethal pressure along the second rank.

16...♖b8 17.♗xa6 ♖xb2 18.♗e2 ♘xf3+ 19.♘xf3 ♗xf3 20.gxf3 ♕g5+ 21.♔h1 ♗xf2 22.♖f1 ♕e3 23.♗c4 ♖d2 24.♕b3 ♕f4 25.♖ad1

25...♖xd1?!

It turns out that 'rook' can also be confusing. The rook move in the game keeps Black's advantage, of course, but Sofia had meant 25...♖b2!, which wins quickly. The rook is taboo because of mate on f3,

while after queen moves along the third rank a bishop retreat would threaten mate on h2, e.g. 26.♕c3 ♗d4!. And even though Black was much better for a long time after this last inaccuracy, what Yona complained about was precisely missing this nice idea.

26.♖xd1 ♔h8 27.a4 ♗b6 28.♗e2 f5

Around this point, both teams had less than a minute left, and the game continued as a blitz between Matthew and Yona.

29.♕c4 fxe4 30.♕xe4

30...♕g5

Since Dracarys needed a draw to win the final, a more practical decision was swapping the queens with 30...♕xe4 and preserving a

considerable advantage at no risk.

31.♗d3 g6 32.a5!? ♗c5

Once again, playing for a queen swap would have been safer: 32...♗xa5 33.♖g1 ♕f5.

33.a6

The position is now far from clear already, and Matthew proved more inspired in the final phase.

33...♕f6 34.♖f1 ♔h7 35.♕b7 ♕d4 36.♕xc7+ ♔g7 37.♕c6 ♖f7 38.♕e4 ♕f6 39.f4 ♔g7 40.♔g2 ♖e7 41.♕d5 ♕b2+ 42.♔h1 ♕d2 43.♕f3 ♖e3 44.♕b7+ ♔f6 45.♗c4 d5 46.♗xd5 ♖e7 47.♕c6+ ♔g7 48.♕xc5 ♖d7 49.♗g2 ♕e3 50.♕xe3 1-0.

Tied at 1-1, the match entered the sudden-death phase, which was once again entertaining and dramatic. The Game Changers had the white pieces, but Dracarys eventually prevailed and were proclaimed the tournament winners.

Summing up

■ In hand-and-brain games, the team spirit is essential, involving a wide palette of elements, such as thinking at the same frequency both strategically and tactically.

■ After this first experiment I believe that hand-and-brain is entertaining and fun for both the players and the audience.

■ The most inspiring words about the experiment came from Vladimir Kramnik. The former World Champion expressed his intention to try a hand-and-brain game with his wife, right after returning home. ■

Never-ending

Endgames, you have to work on them; there's no way around it. Even if you know certain endgame rules, applying them in practice requires, eh, practice! **MAXIM DLUGY** draws endgame lessons (and useful conclusions!) from the Superbet Blitz in Bucharest.

The sixth leg of the 2019 Grand Chess Tour, the Superbet Blitz and Rapid in Bucharest, was won by Levon Aronian. Yet, for me, the real star of the event was Sergey Karjakin, who came from behind after the Rapid portion to shine in the Blitz. The Russian scored a resounding plus-4 in this stellar field and eventually shared first place with Aronian. While the tour points and prize-money were split, a play-off of two games, with a compromise 10 plus 5 time-control, decided on the champion of the Bucharest event. It was here that the Armenian prevailed by winning the second game.

The focus of this instalment will be on what we can learn about the endgame from top blitz tournaments and what traits make for a better endgame player in fast time-controls. We start with a game between Fabiano Caruana and Wesley So and pick up their battle at a point at which Fabiano had compromised his pawn structure and found himself in the following rook-and-pawn ending.

Fabiano Caruana
Wesley So
Bucharest blitz 2019 (3)

position after 33...♖xe8

White now faces a tough choice:
– Trade rooks and counterattack the b-pawn;
– Trade rooks and defend the c-pawn;
– Keep the rook on e3 and defend it with your other rook.
Before looking at Caruana's move, stop to think about which of those choices you would pick and why.
34.♖xe8
Unfortunately for White, all the choices are pretty bad. But the reasons are quite instructive:

34.♖de1 looks like the best option, since it will restrict the ability of Black's king to come to the queenside. Unfortunately, it does the same for White's king if Black plays correctly. After the strongest move, 34...♖a2+,

ANALYSIS DIAGRAM

35.♖1e2 is the most principled variation, because if White can hold here, he should be OK in the rook-and-pawn ending.
Instead, after 35.♔f1 ♖xe3 36.♖xe3, there is 36...♖h2.
And after 35.♔g3 ♖xe3 36.♖xe3

ANALYSIS DIAGRAM

36...g6! White is hard-pressed to find counterplay and Black will eventually swing the king to the queenside. For example: 37.♖e1 ♖a3 38.♖b1 ♖b3 39.♖c1 ♔e6 40.♔f2 ♔d5 41.♔e2 ♖b2+ 42.♔d1 b4, and Black's king will win the d-pawn, with a winning game.

34...♔xe8

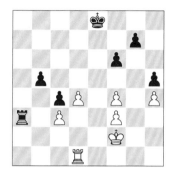

35.♖c1

Counter-attacking the b-pawn with 35.♖b1 actually doesn't make any difference, since Black would simply play 35...♖b3, forcing the game continuation.

35...♔d7

Black strengthens his position with natural moves, while White can only helplessly watch his position collapsing move by move.

36.f5 ♔d6 37.♔e2 ♔d5 38.♖c2 ♖b3 39.♖c1 b4 40.cxb4 ♖xb4 41.♖g1 ♖b7 42.♖d1 ♖e7+ 43.♔d2 ♔xd4 44.♔c2+ ♔c5 45.♖d8 ♖e2+ 46.♔d1 ♖h2 47.♖g8 ♖xh4 48.♖xg7 ♖f4 49.♔e2 ♖xf5 50.♖h7 ♔d4

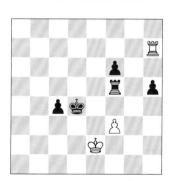

As White resigned, I have a feeling he was thinking he should have tried his luck in the losing but far more complicated king-and-pawn endgame.

Fabiano Caruana and Anish Giri are cornered by young autograph hunters in Bucharest.

LENNART OOTES

Moral: when faced with a hopeless passive defence or a dynamic but bad endgame – choose the latter; it will be your best chance.

Assessing the real threats

Anish Giri
Fabiano Caruana
Bucharest blitz 2019 (4)

position after 65...♗h6

After a lot of manoeuvring in this interesting endgame, Fabiano Caruana decided to offer a bishop swap, banking on the beautiful position of his rook on e4, and on having more space on the queenside. Stop to think what White should do now:

1. Trade bishops?
2. Play a waiting move and allow the trade on f4?

66.♖f1? A clear mistake. White should have traded bishops himself. After the natural 66.♗xh6 ♖xh6 67.g4! White clears the kingside quickly and fully equalizes. Now White gets himself into trouble.

66...♗xf4 67.gxf4 ♔f6

The main issue is that White has no way to meet Black's pressure on the e-file, as his h-pawn is hanging on h4.

68.♖d1 ♖he7 69.♖d3

When faced with a hopeless passive defence or a dynamic but bad endgame – choose the latter.

69...♖e2?!

An even simpler way to win without allowing counterplay was 69...♖e1! 70.♖xe1 ♖xe1 71.♖e3 ♖a1, and with the capture of the a-pawn, Black's advantage becomes decisive.

70.h5! White correctly judges that he must look for some counterplay, and he looks for it by trying to get his rooks closer to Black's king.

70...♖a2? This move throws away the win, since White's counterattack is good enough to counteract Black's threats. 70...♖e1! was still good enough to win quite easily.

71.hxg6?

Anish misses the draw with this move. The h-pawn is what he should have banked on. After 71.h6! ♖h7 72.♖e3 ♖xa3 73.♖he1 ♖xh6 74.♖e6+ the game would end in a draw by perpetual check. Now, after White's capture on g6, Black should have asked himself a simple question: What's my opponent's threat? And since there was no real threat, he should have continued with his idea.

71...♔xg6?

Fabi misses his chance to win and allows White saving counterplay. Black wins after 71...♖xa3, threat-

ening 72...b4, since White simply has no way to follow up with any active ideas here.

72.♖dd1!

The rooks are now strong enough to secure a draw in all variations.

72...♖g7 Instead, after 72...♖xa3 73.♖dg1+ ♔f7 74.♖h7+ ♔e8 75.♖g8+ ♔d7 76.♖hh8 ♖xc3+ 77.♔f2 ♔e6 78.♖c8 ♔f6 79.♖xc6+ ♔g7 80.♖h5 White has sufficient play to survive.

73.♖de1

A bit too optimistic. There is no reason not to trade the rook on the second rank now with 73.♖a1 ♖c2 74.♖ac1 ♖xc1 75.♖xc1, with a pretty clear draw.

73...♔f7 74.♖h5

74...♔g6 After 74...♖xa3 75.♖xf5+ ♔g8 76.♖e8+ ♔h7 77.♖h5+ ♔g6 78.♖eh8 ♖xc3+ 79.♔f2 a3 80.f5+ ♔f7 81.♖c8 a2 82.♖c7+ ♔f8 83.♖c8+ ♔f7 84.♖c7+

ANALYSIS DIAGRAM

White draws easily.

75.♖h8 ♖xa3 76.♖e6+ ♔f7 77.♖xc6 ♖xc3+ 78.♔f2 a3 79.♖c7+ ♔g6 80.♖c6+ ♔f7 81.♖c7+ And the players finally agreed to a draw.

As you can see, a correct assessment of the real threats could have helped both players. Black missed his chance to trade a set of rooks when White had no counterplay, while White underestimated the strength of his h-pawn and once again found himself in a lost position. Black responded by failing to see that his opponent didn't have any real threats and opened up his king by taking the g6-pawn. Correctly assessing *real* threats is, therefore, a major strength in endgames.

Active rooks

Vladislav Artemiev
Anton Korobov
Bucharest blitz 2019 (4)

position after 41...♖d5

In this tense game between Vladislav Artemiev and Anton Korobov it is clear that Black, who earlier on had won the isolated d-pawn, is playing for a win. In such situations, Black must be careful not to lose his extra pawn or to get as much as he can for it, as otherwise the advantage will disappear.

42.♖c4

Now Black has a choice between supporting his e4-knight with the pawn and looking for a better square for the knight. Which option would you choose?

42...f5?

Although the knight stands beautifully on e4, the poor position of Black's king allows a simple fork. It was necessary to play 42...♘c3 43.♖d2 g5!, gaining more space, and

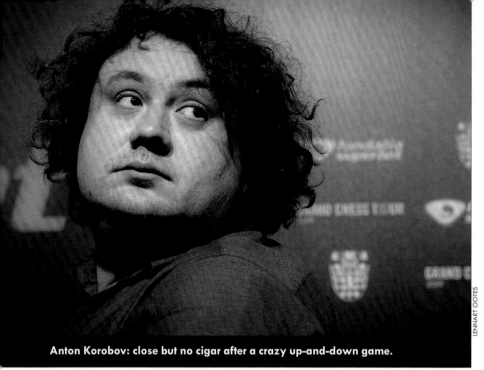

Anton Korobov: close but no cigar after a crazy up-and-down game.

47.♔f3 ♔f6 48.♔e4 ♖d6 49.♔f3, and it's not at all clear how Black could improve his position when the king has no entry squares and the rook on b7 is confined to defending the b-pawn.

45...♔g7

46.h5?! This move creates a potential weakness on h5 for White. White had to carry out a clear-headed plan as above to keep the balance. For example: 46.♖c4 ♔f6 47.f3 ♖d6 48.♔f2, and he should draw.

46...♖e7 47.♔f1?!

After this passive move White will be hard-pressed to save the game. The strongest way to resist was 47.f4! gxf4 48.gxf4 ♖e4 49.♔f3 ♖dd4 50.♖g2+ ♔f7 51.♖c7+ ♔f8 52.♖c5 ♖xf4+ 53.♔e3

ANALYSIS DIAGRAM

and the activity of White's rooks will save him after 53...♔e7 54.♖xf5 ♖xf5 55.♔xd4 as 55...♖xh5 56.♔xd3 ♖h3+ 57.♔c4 ♖h4+ 58.♔d3, when the position is objectively drawn.

47...f4! The reason that 46.h5 was a mistake is getting clear. If White captures on f4, the h5-pawn will become a direct target.

White cannot win the pawn for free, because after 44.♘d4 ♘e4 45.♖xd3 gxh4 46.gxh4 ♘d6 47.♖c6 ♖d7

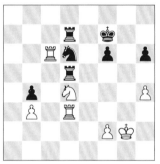

ANALYSIS DIAGRAM

the pin on the d-file will net Black at least an exchange, with good winning chances after 48.♖b6 h5 49.♖d1 ♘f5 50.♘xf5 ♖xd1 51.♖xb4 ♖1d3.

43.♘d2? Amazingly, in the heat of the battle Artemiev misses the simple 43.♖xd3 ♖xd3 44.♘e5+, with

equality. Always look for captures and checks in blitz, especially in endgames, since it is 1. easy to do, and 2. more effective, because there are fewer pieces on the board.

43...♘xd2?

This is a typical mistake. Rook-and-pawn endings are notoriously difficult to win, even with an extra pawn, and if Black has a viable option to keep the knights on the board, he should definitely go for it.

After 43...♘d6 44.♖c6 ♖e7 45.♘c4 ♘e4 46.♘e3 ♖dd7 47.♘xf5 Black's d-pawn has a career after 47...♘c3! 48.♖a1 ♖e6, and Black wins.

44.♖xd2 g5

45.♖c6 Black's position is no longer winning, but as we will see, the possibilities for making mistakes in rook-and-pawn endgames are well-nigh endless. The simplest way to equality could be 45.hxg5 hxg5 46.g4 f4

48.♖g6+

To save the game here, White would have to find the non-human 48.f3! fxg3 49.♔g2, getting some much-needed activity for his king.

48...♔h7 49.gxf4 gxf4 50.♖f6

50...♖e4?!

In chess it's very important to optimize. On d4, the d-rook would defend both the d3- and f4-pawns, leaving the other rook to do damage. The difference is quite striking. After

50...♖d4! 51.♖f5 ♔g7 52.f3 ♖g3 53.♔f2 ♖g5 54.♖f7+ ♔g8 55.♖c7 ♖xh5 Black has a simple win.

51.♖f7+?! The last chance for counterplay in this position was 51.f3! ♖ed4 52.♖f7+ ♔g8 53.♖e7 ♖xh5 54.♖a2! ♖d8 55.♖aa7 ♖g5 56.♖ad7 ♖xd7 57.♖xd7 ♖e5 58.♖xd3 ♖e3 59.♖d4 ♖xf3+ 60.♔e2 ♖xb3 61.♖xf4, although objectively Black is winning here as well.

51...♔g8 52.♖c7?! f3!

Active rooks are usually worth more than an extra pawn.

The game is nearing the end, and it seems unlikely that White will survive.

53.♖a2

Now take a minute to decide which rook to drop back to the eighth rank to finish the game promptly. If you chose 53...♖d8!, you were absolutely right.

53...♖e8? Now the game flared up again, while after the correct 53...♖d8! the engine announces mate in 16 and Black wins. For example: 54.♖aa7 d2 55.♖g7+ ♔f8 56.♖af7+ ♔e8, and the key detail is pretty clear in this position – the e4-rook stops ♖e7 check. Such is not the case after Anton Korobov's blunder.

54.♖aa7 ♖g5

55.♖e7? White fails to find a convincing way to save the game. After 55.♖h7! ♖c8 56.♖hc7 ♖xc7 57.♖xc7 ♖xh5 58.♔e1 ♖h1+ 59.♔d2 ♖b1 60.♔xd3 ♖xb3+ 61.♔e4 the active position of the king saves him: 61...♖b2 62.♔xf3 b3 63.♖b7, with a draw.

55...♖xe7 56.♖xe7 ♖xh5 57.♔e1

57...♖h1+?

The difference between the rook being on c7 and it being on e7 could have been exploited decisively by Black with 57...♖c5 58.♔d2 ♖c3 59.♖d7 ♖xb3 60.♔e3 ♔f8. The extra pawn compared to the above line decides the position in Black's favour: 61.♖b7 h5 62.♖d7 ♔e8 63.♖h7 ♖b2 64.♔xd3 ♖xf2 65.♔e3 ♖h2 66.♖b7 ♖b2 67.♔xf3 b3 68.♔g3 ♖b1 69.♔h2 ♔d8,

ANALYSIS DIAGRAM

and the Black king will approach the b1-square without playing the pawn to b2.

58.♔d2 Now this complicated endgame peters out to a draw.

58...♖b1 59.♔xd3 ♖xb3+ 60.♔e4 ♖c3 61.♖b7 ♖b3 62.♔f4 ♔f8 63.♔e4 ♔e8 64.♖h7 ♖c3 65.♖b7 b3 66.♔d4 ♖c2 67.♖xb3 ♖xf2 68.♔e4 Draw.

It goes without saying that many of the nuances of this endgame could not be correctly assessed in a blitz game, but there were a few key ideas that I think we can definitely note:

① If you have an extra pawn, try to avoid a pure rook-and-pawn ending, because those endgames are notoriously difficult to win.

② Always look for activity for your rooks. Most of the time, active rooks are worth an extra pawn or more.

③ Look for the key threat posed by your opponent. Spot the square you need to protect to defuse it.

Pawn structure judgement

Quite an instructive endgame occurred in one of the blitz games between Le Quang Liem and Vladislav Artemiev.

Le Quang Liem
Vladislav Artemiev
Bucharest blitz 2019 (5)

position after 32...exf4

In this position, Black should strive to create counterplay on the queen-side to force White on the defensive before the reverse happens to him. When Black ignored the possibility

that White can clamp him down, he was outplayed quite quickly. Watch and learn!

33.♔d3 ♖c5 33...a4 was possible, securing counterplay on the queen-side as needed. After 33...a4 34.b4 a3 35.♔d4 ♔f6 36.♖c3 ♖a4 37.♖b1 neither side can really start anything, and the position looks drawn.

34.♔d4 After 34.a4 Black should act quickly to create something of a blockade on the kingside with 34...h5 35.♗f3 ♖e5, with an equal game

34...♖a7 35.♖c3

35...♖ac7? This is already a serious mistake, as White demonstrates with resolute play.

Black should have started his counterplay with 35...b5! 36.cxb5 ♖xb5 37.♖c7+ ♖xc7 38.♖xc7+ ♔f6 39.♖d7 ♖b6 40.♖a7 ♖b4+ 41.♔d3 ♖b5, with an equal game.

36.a4! Suddenly the clamp is on. Black no longer has a simple solution, since White is threatening to open the h-file and invade after ♖f3, either winning the pawn or forcing ...g6-g5.

36...♔f6? This walks right into the line of fire. After the relatively best 36...♗e6 37.♗xe6 ♔xe6 38.♖f3 g5

39.♖h1 ♖e5 40.hxg5 hxg5 41.♖h6+
♔e7

ANALYSIS DIAGRAM

White has a number of ways to use his active rooks, although with optimum play, Black should probably hold.
37.♖f3! g5 38.hxg5+ hxg5 39.♖h3

39...♗g6?! It's never too late to get active. Again, Black's best chance was 39...b5 40.axb5 ♖xb5 41.♖a1 ♖e5 42.f3 ♔g7 43.♗f5 ♖ec5 44.♖h7+ ♔f8 45.♖h8+ ♔e7 46.♖a8 ♖b7 47.♔c3 ♗e6 48.♗xe6 ♔xe6, even though his troubles aren't over after 49.♖h1!.
40.♖ch1 ♖e7 41.f3 ♖cc7

42.♖h8 42.♔d5! was even stronger, but there's no reason to complicate things in a blitz game.

Le Quang Liem shared first in the Superbet Blitz with Sergey Karjakin.

42...♖h7 43.♖1xh7 ♗xh7 44.♖b8 ♔e7 45.♖xb6 ♗g8 46.♖b5 ♔f6 47.♖xa5 ♖h7 48.♖f5+ ♔g6 49.a5 ♖h1 50.♖f8 ♔g7 51.♖d8 ♖a1 52.♖d7+ ♔f8 53.♖a7 ♗f7 54.a6 ♗e8 55.♔d5 ♖b1 56.♔xd6 ♖xb3 57.♖a8 ♖b6+ 58.♔c5 ♖c6+ 59.♔d5 ♖b6 60.♗h5

Black resigned.

As you can see, recognizing the nature of the pawn structure is extremely important in endgames. White was the first to imagine that with the queenside locked only he would be able to get active on the kingside. That saved him valuable time in making his moves and got him a nearly decisive advantage, forcing Black to spend time looking for defensive moves. Pawn-structure judgement should not be underestimated in blitz!

Dead-drawn, but

The following game between Wesley So and Le Quang Liem was a bit of a tragicomedy. White misplayed the middlegame and wound up in an endgame a pawn down. But in a position with many pawns and four minor pieces, he put up a staunch defence and managed to steer his way into a dead-drawn endgame.

Let's see how difficult it is to navigate even in a dead-drawn position with little time on your clock.

Wesley So
Le Quang Liem
Bucharest blitz 2019 (6)

position after 48...♞e6

49.h4 This makes sense, but a less resolute and safer approach would be to prepare h4 by walking the king to g3. **49...gxh4 50.♔f3 ♔g5 51.♔g2 ♞f4+ 52.♔h2 h6 53.♗f3 ♞g6 54.♗e4 ♞e5 55.♗a8 ♔g4 56.♗d5 ♞d3 57.♗e6+ ♔g5 58.♗d5**

58...h3! Although this move basically nullifies his attempt to play for a win, the tactical fork idea on f4 forces White to give up precious seconds

and creates real practical chances. **59.♗b7?** We can see the result of the shock by this move. After 59.♗e6 it would have been an automatic draw. Nothing has been ruined of course, but we are talking practical chances...
59...♚h4

60.♗c8??
Now this natural move simply loses! White's problem is that only two moves actually draw here, since Black is threatening ...h5 and ...♘f2-g4. 60.♗a6 ♘f2 61.♗e2 h5 is met by

62.♗xh5 ♚xh5 63.♚g3, with a draw, while 60.♗f3 ♘f2 61.♗e2 leads to a position similar to the previous one. As you can see, White had to recognize this drawing idea to survive this endgame. I imagine one (well, players of this calibre) would need between 20 and 30 seconds to figure it out.

60...♘f2! The problem is that the pawn going to h5 will allow Black to check with ...♘g4, forcing the White king back, after which it is a trivial win, since the White bishop and king

are treading on each other's toes.
61.♗e6 h5 62.♚g1 ♚g3
White resigned.

Conclusion
As we have seen from the analysis of these endgames, a number of key factors would lead to a significant improvement in endgame strength:

1 A knowledge of typical winning and drawing positions;

2 Understanding when to complicate instead of waiting for the inevitable to happen in a bad position;

3 Looking for rook activity at all cost. Active rooks are usually worth more than an extra pawn;

4 Understanding the real threats of the position and defending only against the real threats. ■

Such energetic play!

His style is bedazzling and he seems to have the extraordinary talent that marks great champions. At the Hoogeveen chess festival in the north of the Netherlands, **JAN TIMMAN** was impressed by the performance of 16-year-old Alireza Firouzja from Iran. And he spotted a couple of other up-and-coming youngsters.

With both the Grand Swiss in the Isle of Man and the European Team Championships taking place at the same time, tournament director Loek van Wely did not have it easy this year to find interesting players for the Hoogeveen Chess Tournament. Particularly for the two six-games matches that are the main attraction of the event.

Originally, I was scheduled to play Lucas van Foreest, but then Lucas became Dutch champion and felt obliged to defend the national tricolour in Batumi. Van Wely found a replacement in 19-year-old Zhansaya Abdumalik from Kazakhstan, who is the world's strongest under-20 female player.

For the second match, Van Wely also netted two interesting stars. 24-year-old Jorge Cori is the strongest player of the South-American continent, while 16-year-old Alireza Firouzja from Iran has been topping the 2700 barrier for a good while and is the second highest-rated player on FIDE's junior list, behind China's Wei Yi. For me it was a pretty strange experience: not only was I the only European in the tournament, but I was also older than the other three players combined!

Everyone was looking forward to Firouzja's performance. Three years

ago, Ivan Sokolov had already told me that the young Iranian was 'World Champion material'. These were his words. And he could know, because he had trained Iranian junior players for years. I was surprised, because in those days, most attention went out to Parham Maghsoodloo, who was three years his senior.

Firouzja had come to Hoogeveen with his father, and like me, they were staying in the Spaarbank-hoeve Hotel, situated in the woods surrounding the town. This gave me the chance to talk to Firouzja's father a few times. He told me that they were living in Paris, which I thought was a good thing. He also asked me for advice: his son did not have a trainer, and would it be better to get a young person or a slightly older one, and did I have any recommendations? Since he had asked me earlier if I did training work, I might have construed this as a veiled job offer. But honesty required me to say that this was not the job for me. Opening preparation has become too onerous a job. In the past, you

could study variations and then rely on your insight during the middle-game. But the computer is relentlessly demanding: everything must be investigated down to the last detail, and there is barely room for doubt or inspiration. I had already had my hands full preparing for my match against Abdumalik.

I told Firouzja's father that I thought an older trainer would be better, but who? That question I was unable to answer. The problem is that the experienced grandmasters of yore are eminently able to give good advice, but young players can work more efficiently with computers.

Taking major risks

I was actually surprised that Firouzja did not have a trainer, but when I saw him at work in Hoogeveen, I realized that he won't need one in any hurry. It had been years since I had seen such energetic play! As White, he absolutely steamrolled Cori in the first game, and as Black he launched into a complicated middlegame combination that entailed major risks.

Jorge Cori
Alireza Firouzja
Hoogeveen 2019 (match-2)

Black is fine. There is no real need for hyper-sharp play. But Firouzja gives in to the temptation.

16...g5!? 16...e4 would have given Black excellent play without many complications, as witness 17.♗xf4 exf3 18.♘xf3 ♗g4 19.♘d2 ♗xc3 20.bxc3 ♕xd5 21.c4 ♕c6, with a slight plus for Black.

17.gxf4 exf4 18.♗xb6 axb6 19.♖fe1

19...♗e5!? Firouzja is determined to sacrifice a piece for an attack. If he had taken the knight, the position would have been equal.

20.♘g2 g4

Alireza Firouzja is always looking for adventure and does not shrink back from trying his hand at the Budapest Gambit.

21.♖xe5 Giving back an exchange was unnecessary. After 21.♗e2 f3 22.♗b5 Black would have found it very hard to justify his piece sac: 22...♕d6 is met strongly by 23.♘f4!, e.g. 23...♗f5 24.♖xe5 ♖xe5 25.♕c4, and White has a winning advantage.

21...♖xe5 22.♗e4 f3

23.♘e3? Now Black's courage is rewarded. Stronger was 23.♘f4, to keep the black rook from h5, after which Black could try taking his other rook to the h-file with 23...b5;

but that's a rather slow plan. After 24.♕b4 ♖a6 25.♕d4 White is better.

23...♖h5 24.♕c4 ♕h4 25.♕c7 This is what White had relied on. But Black still has a finesse up his sleeve.

25...g3! The decisive breakthrough.
26.♘f1 This will lose quickly, but 26.♕xg3+ ♖g5 27.♗xf3 ♖xg3+ 28.hxg3 ♕f6 would also have been hopeless in the long run.

26...gxf2+ 27.♔h1 ♖g5 28.♘g3 ♗h3 29.♗xf3 ♖e8 30.♘ce4 ♖xe4 White resigned.

Three years ago, Ivan Sokolov had already told me that Alireza Firouzja was 'World Champion material'.

I consider Firouzja's third win his best effort.

Alireza Firouzja
Jorge Cori
Hoogeveen 2019 (match-3)
Sicilian Defence, Kan Variation
1.e4 c5 2.♘f3 e6 3.d4 cxd4
4.♘xd4 a6 5.♗d3 d6 6.0-0 ♘f6

7.♘c3 Sharper is 7.f4, as played by out-and-out attackers like Velimirovic and Sax. It allows White to throw up a Maroczy bind with c2-c4 later.
7...♗e7 8.♔h1 ♘c6 9.♘b3 0-0
10.a4 b6 White has not played the opening very energetically. With 10...d5 11.exd5 exd5 Black could have solved his opening problems at once.
11.f4 ♗b7 12.♕f3 ♘b4 13.♕h3
White's intention is clear: he wants to advance his f-pawn.

13...♘xd3 This swap could have waited, since 14.e5? is not the way to meet 13...♖c8 in view of 14...dxe5 15.fxe5 ♘xd3 16.exf6 ♖xc3! 17.bxc3 ♘f2+, and Black wins.
14.cxd3 ♖c8 15.♘d4 ♖e8
16.♗e3 The swap on d3 has cost White his bishop pair, but he has

reinforced his centre. The plan is to aim for the advance f4-f5.
16...♗f8 17.♖ad1 g6

18.f5! Now Firouzja is in his element. **18...exf5 19.♗g5 ♗g7**
20.exf5

20...♕d7! A strong defensive move. Black pins the white f-pawn.
21.♕h4 ♘h5 22.f6
It looks as if Black is going to be hemmed in, but he still has a subtle move to play.
22...h6 Preventing the king's bishop from being locked in.
23.♗d2 His best option.

23...♘xf6 Cori starts an interesting combination, but it's not enough for equality. With 23...♕d8! he would

have more than preserved the balance. Things look dangerous after 24.♘f5, but with 24...gxf5 25.♖xf5 ♖c5 26.♕xh5 ♖xf5 27.♕xf5 ♕xf6 Black can solve all his problems.
24.♖xf6 ♖xc3 25.bxc3 ♗xf6
26.♕xf6

26...♗xg2+ This was the idea; the white rook is unprotected.
27.♔xg2 ♕g4+ 28.♔f2 ♕xd1
29.♗xh6 ♕e1+ 30.♔g2 ♕e5
31.♕f3

The complications are past, and White has the best prospects.
31...b5 32.axb5 axb5 33.♗f4
♕c5 34.♕c6! After initially sidestepping the queen swap, White now offers it himself, because now it would be very good for him.

34...♖e2+

And now it's Black who balks at the idea. But 34...♖d8!, covering the d-pawn, would have been better. Interestingly enough, both players continue to offer a queen swap, but only if the other player does the swapping. After 35.♗e3 ♕e5 36.♕e4 ♖e8 White is finally forced to accept it. After 37.♕xe5 ♖xe5 Black has good drawing chances.

35.♔g3 ♖e1 36.♕xd6 ♕xc3 37.♘f3 ♖e8 38.♕d7 ♕c8 39.♕xb5 f6 40.h4 Preventing the advance of the g-pawn. **40...♕e6 41.d4 ♖d8 42.♕a5 ♖d7 43.♕a8+ ♔g7 44.♕b8 ♕e7**

Black still has a fairly solid defence. Firouzja continues his patient manoeuvring.

45.♗c1 ♔h7 46.♗d2 ♕f7 47.♗b4 ♔g7 48.♗d6

48...♕e6?

A serious error. Black should not have let the white queen occupy f8. With 48...♔h7 he could still have fought.

49.♕f8+ ♔h7

50.♗e5! The death blow. The knight check on g5 cannot be prevented.

50...g5 51.h5 Black resigned.

Budapest Gambit

Three wins straight out of the starting-blocks! A first in Hoogeveen. ChessBase was talking about the 'Firouzja Express'. But in Game 4, the train stalled: Cori hit back. The first draw came in Game 5, after a pitched battle. In the final game, Firouzja struck again after a curious opening choice: the Budapest Gambit. An interesting comparison could be

Firouzja is prepared to try all kinds of positions that promise a good middlegame tussle.

made here with Maghsoodloo, who is prepared to the teeth in many openings and seems to constantly aim for certain types of positions. Firouzja's preparation feels far more playful. He is prepared to try all kinds of positions; not overly long variations in which everything turns on one move, but interesting positions that promise a good middlegame tussle.

**Jorge Cori
Alireza Firouzja**
Hoogeveen 2019 (match-6)
Budapest Gambit

1.d4 ♘f6 2.c4 e5 3.dxe5 ♘g4 4.♘f3 ♗c5 5.e3 ♘c6 6.♘c3 0-0 7.♗e2 ♖e8 8.0-0 ♘gxe5 9.♘xe5 ♘xe5 10.b3 a5 11.♗b2 ♖a6 12.♕d5 ♗a7 13.♘e4 ♖h6

A well-known theoretical position. Black's switch of his rook from a6 to h6 boils down to a temporary piece sacrifice. I found 16 games with this in my database.

14.♕xa5

Strange. We know that White has to capture the knight. After 14.♗xe5 c6 White has the important finesse 15.♗f6!, disrupting Black's set-up. The bishop move was first played in Legky-Gusev, Leningrad 1989, and was seen in practice seven more times. What was Firouzja planning after this? After 15...gxf6 16.♕d3 f5, 17.♘g3 is the most accurate move, after which the game could continue as follows: 17...♗b8 18.♖ad1 d5 19.cxd5 ♕h4 20.h3, and now Black can get a tenable position by capturing twice on g3: the attack has come to a halt.

14...♗b6 15.♕a8 d6 16.c5

16...♕h4! A mere pawn has yielded Black a devastating assault.

17.♗xe5 dxe5 18.f3 A better defensive choice would have been 18.h3, although Black should still be winning after 18...♗d7 19.♕xb7 ♗c6 20.♕a6 ♗xe4 21.♕c4 ♗a7.

18...♕xh2+ 19.♔f2

Zhansaya Abdumalik, the strongest female player under 20 in the world, was on a roll in her match against Jan Timman.

Simply on a roll

My match against Zhansaya Abdumalik got off to a pretty disastrous start: in the first game, I met an inglorious end, and in the second one I got nowhere as White. It didn't make me happy but what can I say? She was simply on a roll. I managed to come back by winning the next two games. In Game 4, Abdumalik betrayed her lack of experience in a rook ending.

Jan Timman
Zhansaya Abdumalik
Hoogeveen 2019 (match-4)

position after 37.♖c2

Black is a pawn ahead, but White's strong centre pawns and centralized king constitute sufficient compensation.

37...♔f6 38.♖f2+ ♔g6 39.♖c2

I considered offering a draw, but then changed my mind. White is in no danger, and I was secretly hoping she would start playing for a win.

39...h5?! And yes! Black avoids repeating moves, but in doing so, she endangers herself. **40.d6!** White could have captured on c3, with a drawn pawn ending. But I was play-

19...♖g6 I think Firouzja was a bit tired here. A far stronger option was 19...♕h4+, forcing the white king back to g1. After 20.♔g1 ♗d7 21.♕a3 f5 22.cxb6 fxe4 Black wins in the attack.
20.♖g1 ♗d7 21.♕a3 ♗h3 22.♗f1 f5 23.♕a4
White's best chance.

23...♖d8?
A shocking mistake that remains unpunished. 23...♔f8 would still have preserved a large advantage, with the game continuing as follows: 24.cxb6 fxe4 25.♕xe4 ♕g3+ 26.♔e2 cxb6. Materially speaking, the position is equal, but Black's pieces have the better coordination.
24.♖d1! Now Black has a serious back-rank problem.
24...♖f8 What else?

25.♕c4+ Here 25.♘g5! could have reversed the roles. After 25...♖xg5 26.♕h4 three of Black's pieces are hanging. **25...♔h8 26.♕f7** This looks good, but turns out to be harmless. **26...♖g8**

27.♘g5 Too late. **27...♖xg5 28.cxb6 cxb6 29.♕c7 h6** Creating a bolthole for his king. **30.♖d8 ♕g3+ 31.♔e2 ♖xd8 32.♕xd8+ ♔h7** White resigned.

ing to win. **40...exd6 41.♔d5**
White is two pawns down, but his passed e-pawn is potentially lethal. Objectively speaking, however, we're still within the drawing margins.

41...g4 41...♔f6 was also possible, e.g. 42.♖f2+ ♔e7 43.♖f7+ ♔e8 44.♖h7, and now Black has the surprising escape 44...♖c4!.
42.e7

42...♖a8? The decisive error. Black should have gone 42...♔f7 or 42...♔f6, forcing White to take the d-pawn. Abdumalik thought that Black was lost after 43.♔xd6 ♖a8 44.♖f2+ ♔g7 45.♖a2. True, the rook has too few back-rank squares, but

with 45...♖xa2! 46.e8♕ ♖d2+ 47.♔c5 c2 she can reach a draw.

43.♔e6!
This is Black's problem. White doesn't take the d-pawn, depriving Black's rook of a check from the side. At the same time, the black king is kept at arm's length.
43...d5 44.♖xc3 h4 45.♖a3 Forcing the black rook to a worse square.
45...♖b8 46.♖b3 ♖a8 47.♖a3 ♖b8

48.♖a4! The most convincing winning attempt. Black's pawns have ceased being threats.
48...g3 49.♖g4+ ♔h5 50.h3 ♖a8 51.♔f7 Black resigned.

LENNART OOTES

13-year-old Javokhir Sindarov from Uzbekistan started with 5 out of 5 in the Hoogeveen Open.

Introducing Javokhir Sindarov
The Open tournament was won by Dutch GM Sipke Ernst. Here, too, youthful talents caught the eye. 13-year-old GM Javokhir Sindarov from Uzbekistan blasted off with 5 out of 5. After a quiet draw in Game 6 he could have struck again in Round 7.

Javokhir Sindarov
Sipke Ernst
Hoogeveen 2019 (6)

position after 24...♖2xb3

White is a pawn up, but his c-pawn is on the way out.
25.e6!? A good move, especially from a practical point of view.
25...♕xc3
Now White will get his way. 25...

fxe6 would have kept Black's defence intact.

26.exf7+ ♔xf7 27.♖d7 ♖8b4

28.♗g5! An interesting queen sacrifice.

28...♕e5? Black was probably unwilling to defend the passive position after 28...♖xa4 29.♖xe7+ ♔g8 30.♖xa4 ♖b8 31.♗h6, but there was no real choice, since the text falls short.

29.♕a2! Introducing a lethal pin.

29...♕xg5

30.♖e1 Time-trouble. With more time, Sindarov would undoubtedly have spotted the crystal-clear 30.♖d3! ♕b5 31.♖xb3 ♖xb3 32.♖b1. White wins a full rook and remains an exchange up in an utterly winning position.

30...♔f8 He must have overlooked this sober reply. His winning chances have gone up in smoke.

31.♖xc7 ♗d8 32.♖xh7 ♖b7 33.♖h8+ ♔g7 34.♕a1+ ♕f6 35.♖xd8 ♖b2 36.♕xb2 ♖xb2 37.♖d7+ ♔h6 38.♖f1 ♕f5 39.♖d4 ♖e2 40.♖g4 ♕c5 41.♖g3 g5 42.♖f3 ♕e5 43.♖b1
Draw.

Viktoriia Kirchei (14) from Russia sensationally gained 166 rating points.

LENNART OOTES

A downright sensation

Sindarov's performance was no real surprise. He had already earned his spurs, despite his youthful age. 14-year-old Viktoriia Kirchei's performance, however, was a downright sensation. The Russian girl started the tournament with a rating of 2051, but stacked on no fewer than 166, helped by the K-factor of 40. In the following game, she takes on a strong young Dutch player that out-pointed her to the tune of 400.

Thomas Beerdsen
Viktoriia Kirchei
Hoogeveen 2019 (7)

position after 27...gxf5

The endgame is equal, but White must be careful.

28.♘f3?
A serious error. Correct was 28.♖ge1, to keep possession of the e-file.

28...♖fe8 29.♖ge1

29...♖e4!
Classical and strong. Suddenly, White is bound hand and foot.

30.♔g1 ♖de8 31.♔f1 a4 32.♗f4

32...a3!
Equally classical. White's queenside is hoovered up.

33.♗c1 ♖xe2 34.♖xe2 ♖xe2 35.♔xe2 b3! 36.bxa3 bxa2 37.♗b2 ♗e7 38.a4

38...♗a3 The final blow, clinching the game. White resigned. ∎

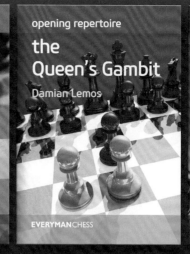
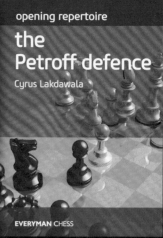
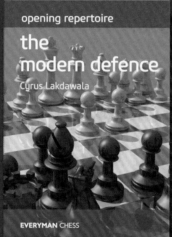
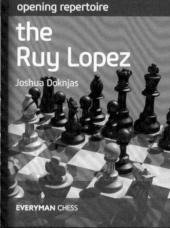

Improving your reservoir of knowledge

The second volume of Gata Kamsky's games collection, a forgotten player from Odessa and more. Prepare for a varied journey as **MATTHEW SADLER** reviews new books.

Franco takes a tour of human experience in this structure from Rubinstein-Schlechter, San Sebastian 1912, to Mamedyarov-Ding Liren, Berlin Candidates 2018, taking in classics by Spassky and Polugaevsky along the way. Without giving you a step-by-step way of playing the positions, it does leave you feeling that you have a good overview of the nuances of Black's two major plans – namely placing the knight on c6 (old-style) or on d7, which both Ding and Kramnik tried in the examples given.

The other chapter I particularly enjoyed was that on 'Space Advantage'. Games such as Adams-Wang Yue

Adams-Wang Yue
Baku Olympiad 2016
position after 18...♖b8

can seem like dry fare when just playing through the moves, but Franco keeps the reader's interest very successfully. I felt that particularly good use was made of comments made by the players after the game. A comment like Adams' really sets the scene well for the technical phase of the game: 'Of course White's advantage is hardly huge here, but I was

The title of Zenon Franco's new book, *Planning, Move by Move* (Everyman Chess), sounded a little contradictory as the goal of planning is somewhat opposite to playing 'move by move'! However, the title refers to a favourite Everyman book format (I think I may have started this trend many years ago with my opening books on the (Semi-)Slav and QGD) which guides the reader through the games and concepts through a series of questions and answers.

The same author produced a fine work on Emanuel Lasker in the same series a little while back. 'First the idea and then the move!' is the subtitle of the book and this catchy phrase of Miguel Najdorf's is 'the perfect summary of planning in chess' according to the author.

The author's approach is to take five common scenarios in which decisions must be taken – the book's five chapters are 'Typical Structures', 'Advantage in Space', 'Manoeuvring Play', 'Simplification' and 'Attack and Defence' – and to present a series of

examples in each scenario. I would characterise the book as inspirational rather than prescriptive, in the sense that after reading the book you can't actually point to any specific new techniques you have learnt (the book doesn't give you any checklists or a specific method for planning), but your reservoir of knowledge has certainly improved.

The first chapter is based around typical pawn structures, mostly from Queen's Gambit openings apart from a 6.♗e3 Najdorf and a Reversed Benoni. The goal of this chapter is to demonstrate that in situations where the pawn structure is one of the most predominant features, it should be easier to select a course of action based on previous experience.

The very first structure Franco examines was at once the most interesting part of the chapter as he considers five examples in the Semi-Tarrasch structure.
1.d4 ♘f6 2.c4 e6 3.♘f3 d5 4.♘c3 c5 5.cxd5 ♘xd5 6.e4 ♘xc3 7.bxc3 cxd4 8.cxd4 ♗b4+ 9.♗d2 ♗xd2+ 10.♕xd2 0-0

**Planning
Move by Move
by Zenon Franco
Everyman Chess,
2019**
★★★☆☆

**Yakov Vilner
by Sergei Tkachenko
Elk and Ruby, 2019**
★★★☆☆

somewhat surprised by how many people considered this a cast-iron draw. When almost everything else is identical, one advantageous feature in a position can quickly magnify in importance and here occupation of

as an illustrious problem composer. The first half of the book is dedicated to Vilner's over-the-board chess activities (including his activities as an organizer and journalist) and the second half of the book deals with

'When almost everything else is identical, one advantageous feature in a position can quickly magnify in importance.'

the e-file and the ability for my rook to also operate laterally should not be underestimated over the board.'

All-in-all, a well-written book that should provide a lot of useful tools and background for club players. It's somewhere between 3 and 4 stars, but we'll stay on 3 this time!

■ ■ ■

Yakov Vilner – First Ukrainian Chess Champion and First USSR Chess composition Champion by Sergei Tkachenko is another interesting offering from the Elk and Ruby publishing house, that specialises in finding and translating unusual Russian-language books into English. The history of chess in Russia is filled with strong players who never played in the West and have remained unknown there. Such a player is the Ukrainian Yakov Vilner, who during his short life (he was dogged by ill-health and died at the age of 31) tied for 6th in the 1924 Russian Championship (won by a rampant Bogoljubow with 15/17!).

Not only was Vilner a strong player, he led an interesting life as a leading figure in the Odessa chess scene and

Vilner's compositions (Tkachenko's own speciality).

Vilner's play was somewhat inconsistent but if you know his name, then you're probably a Semi-Slav Meran player, as he was responsible for introducing this novelty over-the-board (a recommendation of Sozin's) to inflict a rare defeat on Bogoljubow.

**Efim Bogoljubow
Yakov Vilner**
Leningrad 1925
Semi-Slav, Meran Variation

1.d4 d5 2.♘f3 ♞f6 3.c4 c6 4.e3 e6 5.♘c3 ♞bd7 6.♗d3 dxc4 7.♗xc4 b5 8.♗d3 a6 9.e4 c5 10.e5 cxd4 11.♘xb5

11...♞xe5

Bogoljubow had uncorked 11.♘xb5 in the West against Sir George Thomas at Baden-Baden in April of that year and won convincingly. The game A. Rabinovich-Gotgilf had taken place in the 8th round and ended in a convincing win for White. This was hot 1920's theory! It seems that Bogoljubow was taken by surprise by 11...♞xe5.

11...axb5 12.exf6 e5 (12...♗b4+ 13.♔f1 gxf6 14.♘xd4 ♗b7 15.♗e3 ♜g8 16.♜g1 ♗d5 17.♗xb5 ♜a5 18.a4 ♛a8 19.f3 ♛b7 20.♜c1 ♜g6 21.♛c2 ♗d6 22.♛c8+ ♜xc8 23.♜xc8+ ♔e7 24.g3 f5 25.♘c6+ ♗xc6 26.♗xc6 ♞e5 27.♜e8+ ♔f6 28.♗d4 ♗c5 29.♗c3 ♗xg1 30.f4 ♗e3 31.fxe5+ ♜xe5 32.♜b8 ♗c5 33.♜b5 1-0, A. Rabinovich-Gotgilf, Leningrad 1925) 13.fxg7 ♗xg7 14.♛e2 ♛e7 15.0-0 ♗b7 16.♜e1 ♛d6 17.♘h4 ♔f8 18.♘f5 ♛f6 19.♗d2 ♜e8 20.♛g4 h5 21.♛h3 ♗d5 22.♗xb5 ♗e6 23.♛a3+ ♔g8 24.♘d6 ♜d8 25.♘e4 ♛g6 26.♛e7 ♜a8 27.♗xd7 ♗f8 28.♛g5 ♛xg5 29.♗xg5 ♗xd7 30.♘f6+ ♔g7 31.♘xd7 1-0, Bogoljubow-Thomas, Baden-Baden 1925.

12.♘xe5 axb5 13.0-0

13.♗xb5+ ♗d7 14.♘xd7 ♛a5+ 15.♗d2 ♛xb5 16.♘xf6+ gxf6 17.♛f3 ♜d8 18.♛xf6 ♜d5

ANALYSIS DIAGRAM

was Vilner's analysis, when the threat of 19...♜e5+ forces White to tread very carefully!

13...♛d5 14.♛f3 ♗a6 15.♗g5 ♗e7 16.♜fc1 0-0 17.♛h3 h6 18.♗f4 ♗b7 19.♜e1 ♗b4 20.♜e2 ♜xa2 21.♜f1 ♜fa8 22.f3 ♗f8 23.♘g4 ♜xg4 24.♛xg4 ♛b3 25.♗b1 ♜xb2 26.♜ee1 d3

27.♖c1 ♖a1 28.♗c2 ♖xc1 0-1.
A crushing victory and a triumph of 1920's opening preparation!

Even more spectacular are Vilner's compositions. As a composer in his early years, he had a predilection for spectacular queen moves to the corner! I'm slightly spoiling this problem for you by mentioning this, but I did enjoy this one!

Yakov Vilner
Odessa 1913
White to play and mate in 3!

1.♕a1 c3 2.h8♘ ♔e5 3.♘xg6
mate, is the solution! By letting the queen be blocked in the corner, White allows the black king to escape to e5, where it is mated by an under-promoted pawn! Very cool!

A fun book, perhaps slightly stronger on Vilner's compositions than his over-the-board chess (the annotations there are of somewhat variable quality) but wonderful documentation of a chess player and composer who certainly deserves to be better known. Again, this book is somewhere between 3 and 4 stars, but I'll plump for 3 again!

■ ■ ■

The meatiest book this time is *Gata Kamsky – Vol.2 Return (2004-2013)* by Gata Kamsky (Thinkers

The history of chess in Russia is filled with strong players who never played in the West and have remained unknown there.

Publishing). This second volume of Kamsky's best games follows perhaps the most intriguing part of his illustrious career, when he came back after a break of eight years and seemingly picked up effortlessly from where he left off: as a member of the world's elite.

This book consists of 22 densely annotated games featuring impressive wins against a range of the world's best players. The introduction warns that 'this book is not intended as a light read; it contains lots of lines and variations that

**Gata Kamsky Vol.1
Awakening (1989-1996)
by Gata Kamsky
Thinkers Publishing,
2019**
★★★★☆

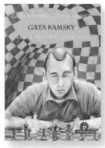

**Gata Kamsky Vol.2
Return (2004-2013)
by Gata Kamsky
Thinkers Publishing,
2019**
★★★★☆

need to be gone over on an actual chess board to understand the point I am making', which sounds quite daunting, even for me! I must confess that I had received the first volume of this three-volume series quite a while back and had found it very difficult to get started. That surprised me somewhat, as I had expected to really enjoy it. As always in such cases, I put the book aside and decided to come back to it once I was in a more receptive mood (yes, even reviewers have their ups and downs). Having been fascinated by Volume II, I went back to Volume I and... I wondered why I hadn't appreciated it the first time!

Firstly, the warning in the introduction is fair: this is not a book you can simply read through and pick up the gist of. It's a book with serious intentions that needs serious and careful study. However, with that caveat there really is a lot to learn. Kamsky is a player of the highest class and the notes are characterised by the patient attention that he gives to each phase of the game, from the opening, all the way through the vicissitudes of complicated middlegames where time-trouble plays a role, to the endgame.

In particular, after reading through his annotations to just one of these games, I felt I had learnt as much about the opening played as if I had studied it for several weeks. Let's give you an example:

**Gata Kamsky
Sergei Tiviakov**
Montreal 2007
Queen's Pawn Opening, London System

**1.d4 ♘f6 2.♘f3 e6 3.♗f4 c5 4.e3
♗e7 5.c3 b6 6.h3 ♗b7 7.♘bd2**

cxd4 8.exd4 d6 9.♗d3 ♘bd7
10.0-0 0-0

A typical position from the London System has arisen. I've played this a number of times in blitz without really having much clue what I was doing! Kamsky's notes do an excellent job of highlighting the richness and possibilities in the position. 'White's main advantage is that he controls more space in the centre. In addition, he can hope to advance his queenside pawns as far as possible to create potential targets in the endgame. One of Black's most obvious plans is to prepare for the ...e6-e5 push thanks to his central majority.'

11.♖e1 ♖e8 12.a4

'The standard move that threatens to gain more space on the queenside by advancing the pawn to a5 and possibly to a6. In addition, it is impor-

tant to note that in such structures, if Black manages to get his b-pawn to b5 and fix White's c3-pawn, Black manages to solve all his problems because of the strong outpost on d5 for his minor pieces.'

I really like comments like this: in a couple of sentences, an outline of a major White plan and the sketch of a scenario that I might want to aim for as Black.

12...a6 13.♗h2

'A prophylactic move. There are different theories on the best location for White's dark-squared bishop, but I believe it really belongs on the b8-h2 diagonal in support of White's queenside expansion.'

Again, born of experience, a very nice reason for where to place your pieces as White.

13...♕c7

'Black is preparing to complete the transfer of the queen to b7, like a Réti opening with colours reversed, where it will be ideally placed to exert influence along the major a8-h1 diagonal, to protect the a6-pawn and prepare the ...b6-b5 break' (we know why the latter is important – MS).

> # With the complexity and depth of the variations given, only stronger players will be able to profit fully from Kamsky's insights but I would recommend it unreservedly to aspiring young players.

Forcing Chess Moves by Charles Hertan New In Chess, 2019
★★★☆☆

'In addition, the black rooks are now connected, and it will be easier for him to prepare ...e6-e5.'
14.c4

'The first critical moment of the game. White decides to proceed with brute force expansion on the queenside, instead of the more typical wait-and-see tactic of hopping around with his knight from d2-c4-e3 etc... Black must decide now whether he wants to allow White's subsequent b2-b4, potentially followed by a4-a5 and c4-c5, or stop it at once.'
14...a5
'I believe this is an inaccuracy as it allows White to transfer his d2-knight to the superior c3-square with a tempo.'
15.♘b1 ♛d8 16.♘c3 d5

'Correct. Black immediately latches

on to White's vulnerable c4-pawn and opens up his e7-bishop.'
17.b3 ♗b4 18.♖c1 ♖c8

Around this shell of comments that I extracted from the notes, Kamsky provides a wealth of variations to support his ideas and judgements, but from the comments alone I felt I learnt an enormous amount.

In conclusion, two books of great quality. I do think that with the complexity and depth of the variations given, only stronger players will be able to profit fully from Kamsky's

Looking through Tal's attacks, it struck me again how often he just captured stuff to keep his attacks going!

insights but I would recommend it unreservedly to aspiring young players, and anyone who is looking for an opportunity to put in some serious chess study! I think I'll have to stop just short of 5 stars, but an easy 4 stars and warmly recommended!

■ ■ ■

I had the strange experience recently while analysing one of Tal's famous victories of struggling to find – actually, even think of – the not-too-difficult path he took to victory.

Mikhail Tal – Geza Fuster
Portoroz 1958
position after 19...♖f8

After some minutes struggling, I eventually hit on the obvious 20.♖xf8+ ♗xf8 21.♛f3 when 21...♖d8 is impossible due to 22.♖xd8+ ♔xd8 (22...♛xd8 23.♛f7+) 23.♛xf8+.

Trying to puzzle out why I had taken so long, it struck me that the basis of Tal's attack was simple captures. I started thinking that my mind was automatically filtering out such possibilities because they were too simple. After all: strong players never just capture stuff automatically: they try and maintain the tension for as long as possible and find subtle ways to force the opponent to waste time capturing! Looking through some more of Tal's attacks, it struck me again how often he just captured stuff to keep his attacks going! A perhaps rather basic insight for an experienced grandmaster to have I'll grant you, but this reminder to look at simple forcing moves was just what I needed. Curing this type of blindness to the forcing and simple is the premise of *Forcing Chess Moves* by Charles Hertan (New In Chess). Hertan calls this looking at the board 'with Computer Eyes' and the whole book is a set of typical themes followed by exercises to help you develop this instinct. Reading through the book. I did wonder whether the definition of 'forcing moves' was being stretched a little too far, but I truly believe that identifying and thinking about forcing moves in positions is an excellent way to discover latent tactical possibilities. In any case, so many great combinations in one book is always fun to read! Good book, 3 stars! ■

They are **The Champions**

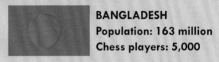

BANGLADESH
Population: 163 million
Chess players: 5,000

Bangladesh Women's Champion Rani Hamid

A bigger contrast is hardly possible. Last time we covered the 13-year-old champion of Belgium. This time, we celebrate WIM Rani Hamid, who this year, at the age of 75, won the Bangladesh Women's title for the 20th time! And this does not even include the three national championships that she won but that were not registered with FIDE.

Rani Hamid (born in 1944) married lieutenant colonel MA Hamid, a sports organizer, at the age of 15. They had three sons and one daughter. Sports took a central place in the family. Kaiser Hamid was captain of the Bangladesh Football Team for many years, Sohel Hamid, a national squash champion, and her youngest son, Boby Hamid, a national handball player.

Rani Hamid only started playing chess when she was 33 years old. Her neighbour at the time was a national chess champion, and that helped her develop quickly. In the 1980s, she won the British Women's Championships three times, and she gained the Woman International Master title in 1985.

The following game fragment is from the match between Bangladesh and Iran at the 2006 Olympiad in Turin. When her opponent gives her the opportunity, Rani Hamid immediately strikes with a tactical shot.

Rani Hamid
Atousa Pourkashiyan
Turin Olympiad 2006

position after 25...d5?

26.♘xf6! gxf6 27.♗xf6+ ♖xf6
28.♖xe8+ ♔g7 29.♕g4+ ♔h6
30.♕h4+ ♔g7 31.♕g5+ 1-0.

Rani, which means Queen in Hindi, has represented Bangladesh 18 times at the Chess Olympiad, including three times in the general (men's) section. Her first Olympiad was in 1984, and since then, she has not missed a single Olympiad. During the 2018 Olympiad in Batumi, she was awarded the Journalists' Choice Award for her many contributions to chess. Three former Women's World Champions, Nona Gaprindashvili, Maia Chiburdanidze, and Susan Polgar supported her nomination.

The grand lady of Asian chess won her national title this year convincingly with 8½ out of 9, even gaining 52 rating points in the process. Titles and ratings are no longer her focus. She stated that she has achieved all she wanted in chess and purely plays for the love of the game, and that she finds joy in playing alongside young talented players. She did, however, set herself a specific goal: to break the record of Edith Price, who became British Women's Champion at the age of 76 in 1948. To achieve that, she will have to win the championship again in 2021 at the age of 77.

Rani Hamid is a big fan of Viswanathan Anand and visited his World Championship match against Magnus Carlsen in India in 2013. More than 35 years ago, she had the opportunity to play against him at the Fakhruddin Ali Ahmed tournament in New Delhi.

'Anand was a young boy, and he was playing at lightning speed; he used to win in no time against his opponents, but our game was taking much longer than usual; I remember his mother getting a bit restless and worried because of that. I was an exchange up at one stage, but Anand, of course, won.' ∎

In **They are The Champions** we pay tribute to national champions across the globe. For suggestions please write to editors@newinchess.com.

Davorin Kuljasevic

CURRENT ELO: 2554

DATE OF BIRTH: October 22, 1986

PLACE OF BIRTH: Zagreb, Croatia

PLACE OF RESIDENCE: Plovdiv, Bulgaria

What is your favourite city?
Biel, Switzerland.

Which book would you give to a dear friend?
Catch-22 by Joseph Heller.

What book is currently on your bedside table?
Something about financial markets, but it is mostly collecting dust, unfortunately.

What is your all-time favourite movie?
I'll go with *The Shawshank Redemption*.

And your favourite TV series?
Several years ago, I enjoyed watching *True Detective* and *Black Sails*.

Do you have a favourite actor?
Robert De Niro.

And a favourite actress?
Not really, but I like Anne Hathaway.

What music do you listen to?
Rock music from the 70s and grunge from the 90s.

Is there a painting that moves you?
Paintings by Mark Chagall and Salvador Dali.

What is your earliest chess memory?
Announcing 'Checkmate!' to my nemesis in a children's tournament, only to discover that the fianchettoed bishop from g7 can prevent back-rank checkmate by moving back to f8.

Who is your favourite chess player of all time and why?
Magnus Carlsen, because the strength of his play continues to impress me.

Is there a chess book that had a profound influence on you?
Think like a Grandmaster by Kotov when I was starting out, and *Endgame Strategy* by Shereshevsky a little bit later.

What was your best result ever?
Winning the Split Open in 2013 with 8/9, a clear point ahead of the field.

And the best game you played?
The final combination of Baron-Kuljasevic, Skopje 2013, stands out for aesthetic reasons.

What is your favourite square?
The c2-square, because two of my opponents blundered a full piece on that square in the same tournament in two consecutive years!

What are chess players particularly good at (except for chess)?
Chess players have better developed abstract thinking than most people.

Do you have any superstitions concerning chess?
I pray to Caïssa every night before the game. Just kidding ☺.

Facebook, Instagram, Snapchat, or?
Facebook.

How many friends do you have on Facebook?
931, just checked.

What is your life motto?
Live and let live.

When were you happiest?
Every time my little baby daughter smiles at me.

When was the last time you cried?
When my father died.

Who or what would you like to be if you weren't yourself?
A world-class football player.

Which three people would you like to invite for dinner?
George Carlin, Craig Ferguson, Joe Pesci.

What is the best piece of advice you were ever given?
Don't listen to other people's advice.

What would people be surprised to know about you?
That I wrote a book on chess! (It is called *Beyond Material*.)

What is your greatest regret?
I believe that everything in life happens for a reason, so I don't have many regrets.

If you could change one thing in the chess world, what would it be?
A life ban for proven cheaters.

What does it mean to be a chess player?
Not having time to rest on your laurels or wallow in self-pity. Every new game brings a new challenge.

Is a knowledge of chess useful in everyday life?
I am sure that it is at least useful for improving the longevity of your cognitive functions.

What is the best thing that was ever said about chess?
'On the chessboard, lies and hypocrisy do not survive long.' – Emanuel Lasker.